THE FORGOTTEN ORDER

Origin. Authority. Destiny.

C. Lee Henry

The Forgotten Order: Origin. Authority. Destiny.
First Edition

Published by The Here Center. https://here.center

Unless otherwise noted, Scripture quotations are from the Berean Standard Bible (BSB).

ISBN: 979-8-9948338-0-3
Cover design by C. Lee Henry.
Printed in the United States of America

Table of Contents

Preface: Why I Had to Write This Book

I never set out to write a book defending the biblical order between man and woman.

For years online, I posted what I saw plainly in Scripture. Man's creational headship. Woman's subordinate role as *ezer kenegdo*. The beauty of order reflecting Christ and the church. I expected disagreement. Truth often offends. But what I found was something deeper and more troubling. Evasion. Distortion. Endless walls of text burying God's Word under philosophy, culture, and selective history.

One exchange stands out. A critic dismissed Paul as "fake," twisting verses while ignoring Peter's witness. They attacked 2 Peter's authorship to dodge my question: "Is Peter a fake apostle too?" No answer came. Just deflection. That silence spoke volumes.

The pattern repeated. Modern culture, saturated with feminism and egalitarianism, reframes God's order as oppression or outdated tradition. Jesus is recast as a proto-feminist. Submission is labeled toxic. Headship is called misogyny. Long arguments overwhelm simple truth, discouraging pushback while the Bible's witness is sidelined. Churches compromise. Families fracture. Fatherlessness spreads. Society decays under inversion.

I understand why many embrace egalitarianism today. In a world scarred by failed fathers, abusive authority, and wrongs against women, "equality" sounds like justice. It promises freedom from pain. Autonomy feels like safety. Feminism offers the illusion of power as a refuge, precisely because sinful men have perverted the safety of submission into the shackles of subjugation. Long arguments claiming hierarchy is "extrabiblical" or "cultural" can sway sincere believers, especially when they lean on philosophy over Scripture.

But this view exchanges God's truth for a lie. It ignores the Bible's witness. Hierarchy is creational. The Fall intensifies it with conflict. Christ redeems it. Modern rebellion replays Eden's deception, leading to chaos. Broken homes. Fatherless children. Church division. Societal decay.

The burden grew heavier with every conversation. I watched good people swallow distortions because the counterarguments were too exhausting. I saw young men emasculated, young women misled, marriages crumbling, churches splitting. Recognizing the decay in the rubble of my own ignorance replicated in the lives around me, I saw patterns. The weight pressed until I could no longer stay silent.

Truthfully, I hesitated to write this book. I saw judgment for my own failings in the eyes of critics before the words were even on the page. I feared my lack of perfection as a believer would disqualify me from presenting the Truth that was evident. I feared the attacks I might receive could shame the name of Christ. I questioned myself, not God.

Then I realized something... Every word of the Bible was written by sinners under the anointing of God. Moses was a murderer. Paul endorsed the death of Christians. Peter denied Christ three times. Yet God used these imperfect men to convey perfect truth when they submitted to His Word. The message doesn't depend on the messenger's flawlessness, rather the veracity of the message.

This book is my response. It lets Scripture interpret itself, using the witnesses principle to affirm hierarchy from Genesis to Revelation. We trace creation's design, the Fall's distortion, unified witness, historical continuity, modern distortions, and practical obedience. Extra-biblical sources reinforce, not replace, Scripture, showing hierarchy is not anachronistic, but apostolic and creation-grounded.

My hope is simple. That you read these pages and see what I finally saw clearly. God's order is not oppression. It is freedom. It is harmony. It is the reflection of Christ and His bride. When we return to it, families heal, churches strengthen, and culture finds its way back from the ruins.

Do you see it?

C. Lee Henry
January 2026

Introduction: A Call to Biblical Clarity

The world is loud with opinions on gender, marriage, and authority. Egalitarianism promises equality but leaves roles undefined. Feminism offers empowerment but fractures families. Even in the church, voices twist Scripture to fit modern sensibilities, claiming hierarchy is oppressive, outdated, or cultural. The noise is deafening, and the confusion is deep.

I understand the appeal. In a culture scarred by failed authority and historical wrongs, flattening roles sounds like justice. Who wouldn't want a world where no one is "over" another? Autonomy feels like safety. "Equality" offers comfort when submission has been abused.

But the Bible doesn't bend to our comfort. It stands as God's unchanging Word, cutting through the noise with clarity. From creation, God established order. Distinct roles for man and woman, reflecting His own nature. This book returns to that foundation, letting Scripture interpret itself.

The key to this clarity is a principle God gave for truth. "A matter must be established by the testimony of two or three witnesses" (**Deuteronomy 19:15**). Jesus affirmed it. Paul applied it. This isn't legalism. It's divine wisdom to guard against distortion. One verse alone can be twisted. But when multiple witnesses agree, truth stands firm. (In ***Chapter 5.4***, we will go deeper into how this principle works in action, applying it to the doctrine of hierarchy itself.)

Throughout this book, every claim about hierarchy. Man's headship. Woman's submission. Their equal value in God's image. Will be established by two or three witnesses from Scripture. No solitary proof. No extrabiblical speculation as authority. Just the Bible speaking for itself, from Genesis to Revelation. Extra-biblical sources, such as early church fathers and historical patterns, serve only as reinforcement, confirming what Scripture already teaches.

The book is divided into seven parts to trace this truth step by step.

Part I explores the divine design in creation. The physical reality of derivation and the theological chain of headship. **Part II** examines the interruption of the Fall, where harmony becomes conflict. **Part III** demonstrates Scripture's unified witness, from Old to New Testament. **Part IV** surveys historical echoes, showing how the early church upheld this order against proto-egalitarian heresies. **Part V** confronts modern distortions and their consequences. **Part VI** offers scriptural models for living the order today. **Part VII** warns of judgment for rejecting hierarchy and casts a vision for restoration.

Why this journey? Because in our age of confusion, we need an anchor. The world offers endless interpretations. God offers certainty. When we return to clear Scripture, tested by witnesses, we find not oppression, but harmony. Not division, but unity in Christ's design.

This is the hermeneutical foundation for everything that follows. Let's begin.

PART I: THE DIVINE DESIGN – CREATION'S ORDER

Chapter 1: Creation's Design - The Physical Reality of Derivation

1.1 - Man's Firstness and Authority

Man was formed first by God, and this order of formation establishes his authority over woman. The sequence of creation is not merely chronological but theological, establishing the man as the source and federal head of the human race.

THE WITNESSES

I. **Genesis 2**
   7: "Then the Lord God formed man from the dust of the ground and breathed the breath of life into his nostrils, and the man became a living being."
II. **1 Corinthians 11**
   8: "For man did not come from woman, but woman from man."
III. **1 Timothy 2**
   13: "For Adam was formed first, and then Eve."

The Cultural Rejection of Order

It's easy to see why many today question or reject the idea that the order of creation gives man authority. In a culture that views sequence as irrelevant and prioritizes equality in every aspect of life, the biblical emphasis on who was formed first can seem arbitrary or unfair. It's comforting to interpret the creation account as merely chronological without implications for roles. Some even suggest the order reflects cultural bias or temporary arrangements rather than divine intent.

Modern readers often argue that "first" does not mean "leader," pointing out that animals were created before humans in Genesis 1, yet humans rule over them. They argue: *If priority in time equals authority, shouldn't the beasts rule the man?* This objection, often used as a "gotcha" to dismantle biblical hierarchy, ignores the vital theological distinctions of **Kind** and **Source**.

Dominion and Derivation

This comparison fails because it ignores the specific decrees of God regarding different kinds of creation. The authority of Adam is not based solely on a clock; it is based on **Dominion** and **Derivation**.

1. **The Mandate of Dominion:** While animals were created chronologically prior to man, God explicitly reversed any implication of authority by issuing a direct command for man to "rule over the fish of the sea and the birds of the air, over the livestock, and over all the earth" (Genesis 1:26). God expressly placed the later creation (Man) over the earlier creation (Animals). No such reversal exists between man and woman. God never commanded the woman to rule over the man; instead, the New Testament affirms that the creation order remains the basis for man's authority (1 Timothy 2:13).
2. **The Theology of Derivation:** The authority of Adam over Eve is based on **origin**. Adam did not come from the animals; he was formed from the dust (Genesis 2:7). However, the woman *did* come from the man. As Paul argues in 1 Corinthians 11:8, "For man did not come from woman, but woman from man." This is the doctrine of derivation. Authority flows from the source to the derivative. The animals are not the source of man, but the man is the source of the woman.

The Apostolic Standard

The Bible repeatedly highlights the formation order as the foundation for man's authority. We cannot dismiss this as incidental detail when the apostles invoke it directly to ground headship and order. Scripture does not treat the timing of Adam's creation as a trivial fact of history; it treats it as the structural basis for authority. Paul's argument in 1 Timothy 2 explicitly ties the prohibition of female authority to the fact that "For Adam was formed first, and then Eve." (1 Timothy 2:13). Let the text speak plainly. Man was formed first, and this priority establishes his superior role.

The Solitude of Authority (Genesis 2)

The narrative of Genesis 2 provides the necessary context for understanding this priority. "Then the Lord God formed man from the dust of the ground and breathed the breath of life into his nostrils, and the man became a living being." (Genesis 2:7). This event occurs in a specific context of solitude and responsibility.

1. **The Reception of the Law** Before the woman was formed, the man was placed in the garden "to cultivate and keep it" (Genesis 2:15). It was to the man alone that God gave the moral law: "And the LORD God commanded him, 'You may eat freely from every tree of the garden, but you must not eat from the tree of the knowledge of good and evil...'" (Genesis 2:16-17). Adam received the command directly from God. He was the original recipient of divine revelation and the guardian of the garden. The woman received the command through the man, establishing his role as her teacher and head from the very beginning.
2. **The Exercise of Dominion** Before the woman existed, Adam began the work of dominion. "And... the LORD God... brought them to the man to see what he would name each one" (Genesis 2:19). The act of naming is an act of authority. By naming the animals, Adam exercised his rule over creation. This occurred while "for Adam no suitable helper was found" (Genesis 2:20). This period of solitude was not a mistake but a design feature; it established the man's

identity and authority independent of the woman, whereas the woman's identity is derived from the man.

The Apostolic Prohibition (1 Timothy 2)

The most direct application of this truth is found in 1 Timothy 2. When Paul forbids a woman "to teach or to exercise authority over a man" (1 Timothy 2:12), he does not appeal to the culture of Ephesus or the lack of education among women. He appeals to the timeline of Genesis. "For Adam was formed first, and then Eve." (1 Timothy 2:13).

The argument is logical and absolute. Because the man was formed first, he holds the position of primary authority. Because the woman was formed second, she holds the position of submission. To reverse these roles is to rebel against the order of formation itself. It is to claim that the second can rule the first, or that the derivative can rule the source. Such a claim is contrary to nature and contrary to God.

No Prejudice

Therefore, we must acknowledge man's firstness with full weight. Accept that God formed him first to hold authority. Embrace this priority as divine wisdom, not human prejudice. The order of creation is the order of authority. To reject man's authority is to reject the significance of God's act in Genesis 2. We must align our families and our churches with this original design, understanding that true harmony comes only when we honor the structure God established in the beginning.

Reflection Questions

1. How does the fact that Adam received the law directly from God (Genesis 2:16) before Eve was created impact his responsibility as the federal head?

2. Why does Paul appeal to the order of creation (1 Timothy 2:13) rather than cultural customs when restricting authority in the church?
3. In what ways does modern egalitarian theology attempt to bypass the clear implications of "man did not come from woman, but woman from man" (1 Corinthians 11:8)?

***On Firstness and Responsibility:** Adam was formed first. He received the law first. He was judged first. Firstness is not just privilege; it is the burden of ultimate accountability.*

***On the Logic of 1 Timothy 2:** Paul's logic is linear. Created first implies Authority. Deceived first implies Vulnerability. You cannot have biblical authority without biblical order*

1.2 - Woman as Subordinate Helper

Woman was created as a helper (*ezer*) suitable for man. This designation establishes her essential equality as a human being while simultaneously placing her in a position of functional subordination, created specifically to aid the man in the fulfillment of his divine commission.

🕮 THE WITNESSES

I. **Genesis 2**
18: "The LORD God also said, 'It is not good for the man to be alone. I will make for him a suitable helper.'"

II. **1 Corinthians 11**
9: "Neither was man created for woman, but woman for man."

III. **Genesis 2**
20: "But for Adam no suitable helper was found."

The "Strong Helper" Objection

It makes sense that people today would question the belief that women's roles are meant to be secondary. In a culture that equates helping with lesser status and prizes independent autonomy, the biblical description of woman as *ezer* can feel limiting or even insulting. It's natural for modern readers to recoil from any term that implies one person was made for the sake of another. This framework affords a certain consolation by aligning with modern egalitarian values, suggesting that any form of hierarchy is a result of human sin rather than divine intent.

Modern egalitarian theology often argues that because God is called *Ezer* (Helper) to Israel (Psalm 115:9), the term cannot imply subordination. They suggest that *ezer* actually means "strong warrior" or "savior," attempting to flip the hierarchy to suggest the woman is the superior or equal savior of the man. This interpretation seeks to remove the "office" of the helper from the structure of authority entirely, detaching the word from its creation context to satisfy cultural sensitivities.

The Purpose of Creation

But the Bible, as God's unchanging Word, defines the role of the helper through the physical reality of creation. We must let the text speak without cultural filters. The Scriptures present woman as a helper created specifically for the man, not merely alongside him. God forms man first, tasks him with the garden, and then creates woman to aid him in his solitary state.

Genesis 2:18 states: "The LORD God also said, 'It is not good for the man to be alone. I will make for him a suitable helper.'" This declaration comes after Adam has received the law and the mission. The woman is introduced as the solution to the man's solitude and the necessary aid for his mission. She is not created to have a separate mission: she is created to join his. This sets the stage for the "Chain of Headship" we will examine in Chapter 2, where the Apostolic witness confirms that the woman's purpose is derived from the man's existence.

Refuting the "God as Helper" Fallacy

The argument that "God is a helper, therefore helpers are not subordinate" acts as a logical fallacy because it ignores the context of the relationship. To determine rank and authority, we must look at the source and the commission.

1. **Context Determines Rank:** When a superior helps an inferior (God helping Israel), it is an act of sovereign grace. When a subordinate helps a superior (an assistant helping a

director), it is an act of service and duty. The word *ezer* defines the function (assistance), not the rank. Rank is established by derivation: man came from God, and woman came from man (Genesis 2:22).

2. **The Apostolic Commentary:** The Holy Spirit, speaking through Paul, settles the debate on rank in 1 Corinthians 11:9: "Neither was man created for woman, but woman for man." Paul explicitly links the creation of woman to her purpose for the man. He does not use the "God is helper" analogy to dismantle hierarchy. Instead, he uses the creation narrative to establish the man's headship. This apostolic authority is equal to the Law (2 Peter 3:16). *We'll explain why in Chapter 5.2.*

The Meaning of Suitable (Kenegdo)

The Hebrew phrase *ezer kenegdo* is translated by the BSB as "a suitable helper." The word *kenegdo* means "corresponding to" or "opposite." This establishes two vital theological truths.

1. **Ontological Equality:** She corresponds to him. She is not a lower creature or an animal: she is of the same substance. When Adam saw her, he declared, "This is now bone of my bones and flesh of my flesh" (Genesis 2:23). She is his equal in essence (Imago Dei), a theme we will explore deeply as an "Ontological Guardrail" in Chapter 3.
2. **Functional Distinction:** She stands "opposite" him to help him. One does not design a helper to replace the head, nor to rule the head, but to complete the head. The very nature of being a "counterpart" implies a distinct, non-identical role within the relationship. This functional subordination mirrors the relationship between Christ and the Father, which we will examine in Section 2.3.

The Naming of the Woman (Ish and Ishshah)

The act of naming is a biblical indicator of authority. In Genesis 2:19, Adam names the animals, exercising the dominion God granted him. Immediately following the creation of Eve, Adam exercises this same authority over the woman, while simultaneously recognizing their shared nature.

"She shall be called 'woman,' for out of man she was taken" (Genesis 2:23).

In Hebrew, Adam constructs her name based on his own. He calls himself *ish* (man) and he names her *ishshah* (woman). This linguistic connection creates a clear theology of derivation.

- **Connection:** By using the root of his own name, Adam affirms that she is humanity. She is not a beast.
- **Authority:** By assigning the name, Adam establishes his position as the head. One does not name their superior. The one who gives the name defines the identity and function of the one named.
- **Derivation:** The text explicitly states the reason for the name is that "she was taken out of man." Her identity is derived from him, just as her physical body was derived from him.

Later, he names her again personally: "Adam named his wife Eve" (Genesis 3:20). He defines her category (*ishshah*) and her personal identity (Eve). She does not name him. This one-way exercise of naming confirms that while they are equal in nature, the man holds the office of authority. This pre-Fall hierarchy refutes any claim that male headship is a consequence of the Fall: it is the architecture of innocence.

The Pre-Fall Office

It is critical to note that Adam was commissioned with a place, a purpose, and a law (Genesis 2:15-17) before the woman existed. He was not an isolated half waiting for a co-pilot: he was the source from whom the woman would be taken, establishing his priority in the order of creation. The woman was provided to complete his capacity to fulfill the mandate to be fruitful and multiply. This hierarchy was designed for harmony, but as we will see in Chapter 4, the Fall would later turn this ordered help into a source of conflict and a desire for control (*teshuqah*).

The chronology of creation is not accidental; it is foundational to authority. Paul anchors the hierarchy not in culture, but in the timeline of God's work: 'For Adam was formed first, and then Eve' (1 Timothy 2:13). The one formed first bears the responsibility of the head; the one formed *from* him bears the duty of the helper. Priority in time establishes priority in rank.

Defining Subordination

We must be careful to distinguish between rank and value. Subordination is not a statement of inferiority; it is a statement of order. To be 'subordinate' simply means to be placed within an order (*taxis*) under a head. This distinction is vital because the hierarchy of the home mirrors the hierarchy of heaven. Christ is subordinate to the Father yet equal in essence. As we will see in the Trinitarian Foundation (Chapter 2.3), submission is not a mark of lesser value but of divine order. Likewise, the woman is subordinate to the man, created 'for the man' (1 Corinthians 11:9) to enable his mission, without diminishing her standing as an image-bearer.

Embrace Divine Design

Therefore, we must embrace woman's role as the 'suitable helper' (Genesis 2:18) without apology. This title describes her function: she supplies the strength the man lacks to fulfill his duty. However, this function necessitates a specific order. Because the woman was created 'for the man' (1 Corinthians 11:9) and 'Adam was formed first' (1 Timothy 2:13), the woman is placed in a position of subordination. She is the glory of the man (1 Corinthians 11:7), designed to follow his lead and support his vocation.

To resist this order is to resist the wisdom of God. He didn't create two heads to rule the garden, nor two leaders to chart the course. He created one head and one helper. The woman's subordination is not a punishment to be escaped but a design to be inhabited, a position of vital power exercised under authority. By accepting her derivation from the man, she fulfills her high calling as the essential provision for the man's labor.

Reflection Questions

1. How does Paul's statement in 1 Corinthians 11:9 ("woman created for man") clarify the definition of *ezer* in Genesis 2?
2. Why is the linguistic connection between *ish* and *ishshah* critical for understanding both equality and hierarchy?
3. How does the fact that Adam was given a mission before Eve was created disprove the idea of an egalitarian "co-mission"?

> ***On the Definition of Helper:*** *A helper is not a slave, but neither is a helper a master. The woman was created to fill a void in the man's mission, not to commandeer it.*
>
> ***On Naming:*** *To name is to define. Adam defined the woman as derived from himself (ishshah from ish), establishing the first hierarchy of human history.*

Chapter 2: The Unbreakable Chain - Theological Confirmation of Headship

2.1 - The Father's Chain of Headship

God : Christ : Man : Woman The Bible reveals an unbreakable chain of headship: God the Father is the head of Christ, Christ is the head of man, and man is the head of woman. This is the Father's Chain of Headship (rule flowing from the Father), and it establishes that hierarchy is not a human invention but a reflection of the Divine nature rooted in the physical reality of derivation.

🕮 THE WITNESSES

I. **1 Corinthians 11**
   3: "But I want you to understand that the head of every man is Christ, and the head of the woman is man, and the head of Christ is God."

II. **Ephesians 5**
   23: "For the husband is the head of the wife as Christ is the head of the church, His body, of which He is the Savior."

III. **1 Corinthians 11**
   8-9: "For man did not come from woman, but woman from man. Neither was man created for woman, but woman for man."

The War on Patriarchy

Many today recoil at the term "patriarchy," associating it exclusively with oppression or tyranny. I understand why. In a fallen world, men have frequently abused their strength to dominate rather than lead, causing deep wounds in women and children. In a culture that idolizes autonomy and views all hierarchy as a power struggle, the biblical assertion of a vertical chain of command feels offensive. It is tempting to soften this reality by redefining terms or claiming these structures were merely cultural concessions by Paul. This view offers comfort to those who wish to avoid conflict with modern egalitarian sensibilities by suggesting that the chain was a temporary social arrangement rather than a design inherent to the creation.

The Divine Hierarchy

But to reject this chain is to reject the very structure of the order God has designed. The Bible speaks with absolute clarity. There is a divinely ordained hierarchy that connects the human order to the divine. (*See Chapter 3 for the ontological guardrail against misreading hierarchy as inferiority.*) It is not a ladder of value, but a chain of function and authority. Paul establishes this order definitively in 1 Corinthians 11:3: "But I want you to understand that the head of every man is Christ, and the head of the woman is man, and the head of Christ is God."

This is the Father's Chain of Headship. It begins with the Father ("God") and descends through the Son ("Christ") to the male ("Man") and finally to the female ("Woman"). We must observe that the Holy Spirit uses the same word, kephale (head), for every link in the chain. If the headship of man over woman is a "cultural relic," then the headship of God over Christ must also be a "cultural relic." To break the bottom link is to dismantle the entire theological structure. The chain is a singular unit: the rule of the Father mediated through the Son to the human order.

Headship : Source and Authority

Paul uses the Greek term kephale (head). While some modern interpreters argue this means only "source" (like the head of a river) to strip it of authority, the context of Scripture refutes this limitation while upholding the truth of derivation.

1. **The Theology of Derivation:** As Paul explains in 1 Corinthians 11:8, "For man did not come from woman, but woman from man." This echoes the physical reality of Genesis 2:22, where the woman was formed from the man's rib. Because man is the source of the woman, he is her head. Authority is not a power grab: it is an ontological consequence of origin.
2. **The Mediation of Authority:** Authority flows from the source to the derivative. In Ephesians 5:23, Paul writes, "For the husband is the head of the wife as Christ is the head of the church." The church does not merely come from Christ: the church submits to Christ. Therefore, biblical headship involves the responsibility to lead and the duty to submit. This is the "Unbreakable Chain" that connects human marriage to the relationship between Christ and His people.

The Trinitarian Model

The ultimate proof that hierarchy does not imply inferiority is found in the Trinity itself. Paul states, "the head of Christ is God" (1 Corinthians 11:3). This establishes the "Ontological Guardrails" we will examine in Chapter 3.

- **Equality of Essence:** Christ and the Father are one (John 10:30). They share the same divine nature. Christ is not ontologically inferior to the Father.
- **Functional Subordination:** Yet, Christ submits to the Father. He came not to do His own will, but the will of the Father (John 6:38). Even in the final consummation of all things, "the Son Himself will be made subject to Him who put all things under Him" (1 Corinthians 15:28).

If submission were degrading, Christ would be degraded. But He is not. Therefore, the woman's submission to the man is not a mark of inferiority but a reflection of the divine order. Just as the Son reflects the glory of the Father while submitting to Him, the woman is the glory of the man (1 Corinthians 11:7) while submitting to him. This hierarchy is the architecture of peace: when the order is followed, there is harmony. When it is broken, there is chaos.

Exposing the Distortion

Critics who attack this chain often claim that Paul's writings are "hard to understand" or restricted to the first century. This attack is precisely what Peter warned against in 2 Peter 3:16, noting that "ignorant and unstable people distort" Paul's letters, "as they do the rest of the Scriptures, to their own destruction." By placing Paul's letters on par with the "rest of the Scriptures," Peter confirms that the Father's Chain of Headship is not a cultural opinion but a divine revelation for all ages. To reject the bottom link of the chain (Man : Woman) is to begin a process of deconstruction that inevitably leads to a rejection of the top link (God : Christ).

No Apologies Given

We must stop apologizing for the order God has established. This is true patriarchy: the rule of the Father extending through the Son to the man, ordering the home and the world. To reject this chain is to invite the societal collapses we will explore in Chapter 7.4. Men are called to lead with the sacrificial love of Christ, and women are called to find strength in corresponding aid under authority. We must embrace this order for divine harmony.

Reflection Questions

1. How does identifying "God" as God the Father in 1 Corinthians 11:3 reveal the literal fatherly (rule of the Father) nature of the chain?
2. In what way does the "Theology of Derivation" (1 Cor 11:8) provide a physical basis for man's authority?
3. Why does 1 Corinthians 15:28 settle the argument that submission is a permanent, divine principle rather than a post-Fall curse?

On the Nature of the Chain: *You cannot break the chain at the bottom without disconnecting from the top. Rejection of male headship is ultimately a rejection of the Father's design.*

On the Trinitarian Model: *Subordination is not a dirty word: it is a divine one. If the Son of God finds it glorious to submit to the Father, it is glorious for the woman to submit to her head.*

2.2 - Refuting Egalitarian and Matriarchal Claims

Egalitarian attempts to flatten role distinctions and matriarchal efforts to reverse them stand in direct opposition to Scripture's repeated witnesses affirming man's headship and woman's submission. The biblical mandates for authority are rooted in the order of Creation and are not cultural customs to be discarded.

🕮 THE WITNESSES

I. **1 Timothy 2**
12-14: "I do not permit a woman to teach or to exercise authority over a man; she is to remain quiet. For Adam was formed first, and then Eve. And it was not Adam who was deceived, but the woman who was deceived and fell into transgression."

II. **1 Corinthians 14**
34-35: "Women are to be silent in the churches. They are not permitted to speak, but must be in submission, as the law says. If they wish to inquire about something, they are to ask their own husbands at home; for it is dishonorable for a woman to speak in the church."

III. **1 Corinthians 11**
3: "But I want you to understand that the head of every man is Christ, and the head of the woman is man, and the head of Christ is God."

Confronting Distortions of Divine Order

The push for complete equality in roles or even female priority often stems from deep cultural wounds and a desire for justice. I understand the appeal. When authority has been abused, erasing distinctions or inverting them can appear as the path to healing and fairness. Voices today insist that hierarchy itself is the problem, or that Scripture's pattern needs updating to reflect modern values. It is natural to want to affirm the value of women by granting them identical functions to men.

The Apostolic Standard

Yet Scripture confronts these views head-on, providing unwavering testimony to God's fixed order. The apostles do not hedge or accommodate. They root prohibitions and commands in Creation and the Fall, not temporary customs.

Consider the weight of these witnesses in context. First, 1 Timothy 2:12-14 forbids a woman from teaching or exercising authority over a man. Paul grounds this prohibition doubly.

1. **Creation Order:** "For Adam was formed first, then Eve" (1 Timothy 2:13). This appeal to pre-fall priority establishes that headship is not a result of sin but of design.
2. **The Fall:** "And it was not Adam who was deceived, but the woman who was deceived and fell into transgression" (1 Timothy 2:14).

This reasoning reaches beyond any local situation in Ephesus; it binds the church in all places and times because the facts of Creation and the Fall do not change.

Second, 1 Corinthians 14:34-35 requires silence and submission in assemblies: "Women are to be silent in the churches. They are not permitted to speak, but must be in submission, as the law says." The reference to "the law" likely points back to the order established in Genesis. While women may prophesy with a covering (1

Corinthians 11:5), showing the restriction targets authoritative speech such as teaching or judging, the principle of submission is absolute. Disorderly questioning dishonors the order.

Prophecy edifies under authority and is permitted to women (1 Cor 14:3; Acts 21:9), while authoritative teaching over men is forbidden (1 Tim 2:12; 1 Cor 14:34). The distinction is not cultural but rooted in creation order.

Refuting the Egalitarian Objection (Galatians 3:28)

Common egalitarian objections fall short against these witnesses. The most frequent argument relies on Galatians 3:28: "There is neither Jew nor Greek, slave nor free, male nor female, for you are all one in Christ Jesus." (*We'll revisit this later*)

This verse addresses **salvation** and inheritance in Christ, not **functional roles**. The context is justification, not administration.

- **Standing vs. Office:** In Christ, a man and a woman have equal access to grace. They are co-heirs. However, equality of standing does not erase functional distinctions. Paul uses the "slave nor free" comparison. While a slave was spiritually equal to his master, he was still commanded to obey his master in the earthly realm (Ephesians 6:5).
- **Apostolic Consistency:** If Galatians 3:28 abolished male/female roles, Paul would be contradicting himself when he wrote 1 Timothy 2 and 1 Corinthians 11. Since Scripture cannot be broken, we must conclude that spiritual equality coexists with functional hierarchy.

Colossians 3:11 provides another witness: "Here there is no Gentile or Jew, circumcised or uncircumcised, barbarian, Scythian, slave or free, but Christ is all and is in all." Paul uses nearly identical language, yet immediately follows it with household commands where wives submit to husbands (Col 3:18) and slaves obey masters (Col 3:22). If "slave nor free" does not abolish positional roles, neither does "male nor female."

Refuting the Matriarchal Objection (Deborah and Priscilla)

Matriarchal readings attempt to elevate specific biblical exceptions into a normative pattern, but they lack multiple witnesses to support a rule of female headship.

- **Deborah:** Egalitarians often cite Deborah (Judges 4) as proof that women should rule. However, Deborah was a judge raised up during a time of national apostasy and male failure. Her role was an indictment on the men of Israel. As the prophet Isaiah declares regarding a people under judgment: 'Youths oppress My people, and women rule over them. O My people, your guides mislead you; they turn you from your paths' (Isaiah 3:12). When men fail to lead, God may raise a woman to shame them, but this is a sign of disorder, not the standard for the church.
- **Priscilla:** The mention of Priscilla teaching Apollos (Acts 18:26) is often used to justify female pastors. However, Priscilla and her husband Aquila "took him aside and explained" (privately), not publicly in the assembly. No witness shows a woman holding ongoing authoritative office over men in the assembly.

Scripture never commands or models woman ruling man in home, church, or society as the standard. Instead, inversion brings strife, fulfilling the friction predicted in Genesis 3:16: "Your desire will be for your husband, and he will rule over you."

Strength Through Order

These distortions ultimately exchange God's wisdom for human reasoning, repeating the primal error of questioning divine command. The fruit is division and weakness where God intends strength through order. We must stand firm on the witnessed truth. Reject the flattening or reversal of roles. Honor man's headship and woman's submission as a divine gift. Return to the pattern that blesses obedience.

Every egalitarian reversal ultimately rejects the Father's Chain of Headship established in creation (1 Cor 11:3; 1 Tim 2:13), substituting human autonomy for divine order.

Reflection Questions

1. Why do Paul's appeals to creation order and the Fall in 1 Timothy 2:13-14 refute the claim that role restrictions were merely cultural?
2. How does the headship chain in 1 Corinthians 11:3 demand visible distinction rather than mutual rule?
3. In what ways does the modern church confuse spiritual equality (Galatians 3:28) with functional identity?

> ***On Equality and Role:*** *Equality of essence does not necessitate sameness of function. The President and a citizen are equal in humanity, but distinct in authority.*
>
> ***On the Fall:*** *Hierarchy is not the result of the Fall; it is the immune system against the Fall. When the order is inverted, deception enters.*

2.3 - Trinitarian Foundation of Hierarchy

The functional submission of the Son to God the Father within the Trinity, with no difference in divine essence, provides the perfect model for man's headship over woman without implying woman's lesser value. Hierarchy is not a consequence of sin but a reflection of the Divine nature.

🕮 THE WITNESSES

I. **1 Corinthians 11**
3: "But I want you to understand that the head of every man is Christ, and the head of the woman is man, and the head of Christ is God."

II. **1 Corinthians 15**
28: "And when all things have been subjected to Him, then the Son Himself will be made subject to Him who put all things under Him, so that God may be all in all."

III. **John 14**
28: "You heard Me say, 'I am going away, and I am coming back to you.' If you loved Me, you would rejoice that I am going to the Father, because the Father is greater than I."

The Fear of Inferiority

Perhaps the most persistent objection to biblical hierarchy is the belief that submission implies inferiority. In our human experience, we often equate authority with superior worth and submission with lesser value. Consequently, many reject the headship of the man because they fear it demeans the woman. They view role distinctions as a power play, assuming that if a woman must submit, she must be less significant than the man. This fear drives the egalitarian impulse to flatten the order of the home and church.

The Divine Pattern

However, Scripture dismantles this fear by pointing us to the highest possible example. In **Chapter 2.1**, we established the structural chain of command: God is the head of Christ, Christ is the head of man, and man is the head of woman. Now, we must look closely at the top of that chain. The Bible reveals a perfect hierarchy within the Trinity where there is absolute equality of essence but a distinct order of authority. The Father is the head, and the Son submits.

If submission were degrading, then Christ would be degraded. But Christ is the King of kings, fully God, yet He submits to the Father. This Trinitarian reality anchors created roles, showing that distinction in function does not mean devaluation of personhood.

Exegeting the Relationship

Paul explicitly links human hierarchy to the divine hierarchy in 1 Corinthians 11:3: "But I want you to understand that the head of every man is Christ, and the head of the woman is man, and the head of Christ is God."

By placing the man-woman relationship in the same sentence as the Father-Christ relationship, Paul establishes the sanctity of order.

- **Equal Essence:** Jesus declares in John 10:30, "I and the Father are one." They share the same divine nature. The Son is not a lesser god.
- **Distinct Roles:** Yet Jesus also declares in John 14:28, "the Father is greater than I." This "greatness" refers to the

Father's authority and office within the Godhead, not a superiority of essence.

Therefore, just as Christ is not less divine than the Father because He submits, the woman is not less human or less valuable than the man because she submits. The order is structural, not a measure of worth.

Eternal Submission

Some argue that Christ's submission was only temporary, limited to His earthly ministry to secure salvation. However, Scripture testifies to an eternal order. 1 Corinthians 15:28 describes the consummation of all things: "And when all things have been subjected to Him, then the Son Himself will be made subject to Him who put all things under Him, so that God may be all in all." This eternal functional submission witnesses that hierarchy within equality is not temporary or post-Fall.

Even in eternity, after every enemy is defeated and history is complete, the Son remains subject to the Father. This is not a punishment or a demotion. It is the harmonious, eternal order of the Godhead. If the Son finds His glory in doing the will of the Father forever, the woman can find her glory in honoring the headship of the man.

Guardrails Equipped

This Trinitarian guardrail prevents two opposite errors. It prevents the man from tyranny, for he must remember that his Head is Christ, who leads through sacrificial love. It prevents the woman from rebellion, for in submitting to valid authority, she mirrors the very nature of the Son of God. Submission is not a mark of weakness. It is a mark of Christlikeness.

Therefore, we embrace hierarchy not as a curse of the Fall, but as a reflection of the Divine nature. Men, exercise headship with the humility of Christ toward the Father. Women, offer submission with the confidence that you are modeling the Son's relationship to the Father. In this order, God is glorified.

The submission of the Son to the Father is the ultimate model for the Father's Chain of Headship (2.1): equality in essence, distinction in role, harmony in order.

Reflection Questions

1. How does the relationship between the Father and the Son refute the cultural claim that "equality means sameness"?
2. In light of 1 Corinthians 15:28, is submission a temporary burden or an eternal virtue?
3. How does viewing submission as "Christ-like" change the way we approach authority in the home?

> ***On the Nature of God:*** *To despise hierarchy is to despise the relationship between the Father and the Son. Order is not an imposition on the Trinity; it is the nature of the Trinity.*
>
> ***On Worth:*** *A subordinate role does not imply an inferior soul. The Son submits to the Father, yet He is God. The wife submits to the husband, yet she is a co-heir of life.*

Chapter 3: The Image of God - Equal Essence, Distinct Roles

3.1 - Genesis 1:27 and 9:6 Exegeted

Ha'adam, Oto, Otam Man and woman are ontologically equal in bearing God's image, possessing identical intrinsic value and dignity. However, the grammatical structure of the creation account reveals that this image was deposited first in the man (*oto*) and then extended to the woman (*otam*), mirroring the physical order of formation and the theological order of glory.

🕮 THE WITNESSES

I. **Genesis 1**
27: "So God created man in His own image; in the image of God He created him; male and female He created them."
II. **Genesis 9**
6: "Whoever sheds the blood of man, by man his blood will be shed; for in His own image God has made mankind."
III. **1 Corinthians 11**
7: "A man ought not to cover his head, since he is the image and glory of God; but the woman is the glory of man."

The Guardrail of Equality

In our defense of biblical hierarchy, we must establish a firm guardrail against the error of devaluation. The subordination of the woman to the man in function does not imply a subordination in essence. This equality is anchored in the *Imago Dei* (Image of God).

Yet, even in establishing this equality, the text upholds the priority of the man.

Exegeting Genesis 1:27

Genesis 1:27 is often cited as proof that there is no distinction between male and female, but a closer look at the Hebrew pronouns reveals a profound order.

"So God created man in His own image; in the image of God He created him; male and female He created them."

We must observe the progression of the Hebrew terms in this verse, which acts as a theological definition of humanity's creation.

1. **"God created man" (*Ha'adam*):** Here, the term *ha'adam* refers to the species, humanity, but it is rooted in the name of the first male, Adam.
2. **"He created him" (*Oto*):** The text uses the singular masculine pronoun *oto* ("him"). This refers specifically to Adam, the male, who was formed first (1 Timothy 2:13). The image of God was deposited in the man before the woman existed. He is the repository of the image.
3. **"He created them" (*Otam*):** Only in the final clause does the text shift to the plural *otam* ("them"), encompassing "male and female."

This sequence is not accidental. It demonstrates that while both possess the image, the man was the primary creation, and the woman receives the image through her derivation from him. They share the same nature (*otam*), but the man possesses the priority of formation (*oto*).

This grammatical shift (singular *oto* to plural *otam*) mirrors the physical sequence of creation: Genesis 2:7 states that "the LORD God formed man (*ha'adam*) from the dust of the ground," while Genesis 2:22 records that "from the rib that the Lord God had taken from the man (*ha'adam*), He made a woman." The singular *oto* in

Genesis 1:27 therefore corresponds to the first-formed man, and the plural *otam* includes the woman after she is derived from him.

Connecting to Paul's Argument

This exegetical nuance explains why Paul argues as he does in 1 Corinthians 11:7. "A man ought not to cover his head, since he is the image and glory of God; but the woman is the glory of man."

Paul is not denying that woman is made in the image of God. He is acknowledging the order established in Genesis 1:27.

- **Man (*Oto*):** Created directly by God, he is the "image and glory of God."
- **Woman (*Otam*):** Created from the man, she shares the image but is the "glory of man."

Thus, the grammatical shift from singular to plural in Genesis 1 confirms the theological hierarchy Paul later defends. The image extends to both, but the flow of glory respects the order of creation.

This glory distinction reflects the order of derivation and headship (man as direct image and glory of God, woman as glory of man), yet both remain bearers of God's image (Gen 1:27), preserving ontological equality while upholding positional order.

The Legal Protection of Life

Despite this functional order, the ontological value of that image is equal. Following the flood, God establishes the death penalty for murder in Genesis 9:6: "Whoever sheds the blood of man, by man his blood will be shed; for in His own image God has made mankind."

The Berean Standard Bible translation here uses "mankind" to translate *ha'adam* at the end of the verse, reinforcing the scope of the protection. The reason murder is a capital offense is that the victim bears God's image. This protection applies equally to men and women. The priority of the man in creation does not grant him a license to harm the woman, nor does it make her life less sacred. Her life is inviolable because she bears the *tselem* (image) of God.

Nature and Structure

Thus, we hold to **Functional Subordination** and **Ontological Equality**. The woman submits to the man not because she is less human, but because God created the man first (*oto*) and then the woman (*otam*) to join him. To deny her equality is heresy, for she is "bone of his bones." To deny her subordinate role is rebellion, for she was created for him. Scripture upholds both the shared nature and the ordered structure.

Woman reflects God through the man. This does not diminish her value but defines her orientation in the created order, just as the Son reflects the Father while remaining fully God.

Reflection Questions

1. How does the shift from "him" (*oto*) to "them" (*otam*) in Genesis 1:27 mirror the sequence of events in Genesis 2 (Adam formed, then Eve)?
2. How does this understanding of Genesis 1:27 support Paul's claim in 1 Corinthians 11:7 that man is the image and glory of God, while woman is the glory of man?
3. Why is the translation "mankind" in Genesis 9:6 important for ensuring that the protection of the *Imago Dei* applies to both male and female alike?

On Grammar: *The Bible uses grammar to teach theology. The singular oto establishes the man as the foundation; the plural otam establishes the woman as his equal counterpart.*

On Glory: *Man reflects God directly as the first creation. Woman reflects God through the man. This does not diminish her value but defines her orientation.*

3.2 - Positional Inferiority, Not Ontological

Woman holds a position of functional subordination to man within the created order while simultaneously possessing absolute ontological equality as a fellow image-bearer of God. The spiritual equality of men and women in Christ (soteriology) does not dissolve the authority structures established by God in Creation (function).

📖 THE WITNESSES

I. **Genesis 1**
27: "So God created man in His own image; in the image of God He created him; male and female He created them."

II. **Galatians 3**
28: "There is neither Jew nor Greek, slave nor free, male nor female, for you are all one in Christ Jesus."

III. **1 Peter 3**
7: "Husbands, in the same way, treat your wives with consideration as a delicate vessel, and with honor as fellow heirs of the gracious gift of life, so that your prayers will not be hindered."

The Confusion of Rank and Value

In **Chapter 3.1**, we established through the Hebrew grammar of *Ha'adam* that both the man and the woman possess the *Imago Dei*. They are of the same essence. Yet a dangerous confusion persists in the modern church. Many assume that "equality" must mean "sameness." They argue that if a woman is equal to a man in value, she must be eligible for the same roles. Conversely, some fear that if a woman is subordinate in role, she must be inferior in value.

This confusion drives the egalitarian rejection of biblical headship. It assumes that authority is a measure of worth. If this premise were true, then any form of submission would be degradation.

Defining the Terms

To uphold the full counsel of Scripture, we must distinguish between two theological categories with absolute precision.

1. **Ontological Equality:** This refers to *being* and *essence*. As proved in Genesis 1:27 and Genesis 9:6, man and woman share the exact same human nature and divine value. The life of a woman is as sacred as the life of a man. In their standing before God as humans, they are equals.
2. **Positional Subordination:** This refers to *rank* and *function*. In the economy of God's design, the woman is placed under the authority of the man. This is not a statement about her capability or her soul. It is a statement about her station.

Consider a military analogy. A colonel and a private are both men. They are ontologically equal. The private is not less "human" than the colonel. However, the private is positionally subordinate. He must obey orders. His lower rank does not diminish his value as a man, but it restricts his function within the unit.

The Egalitarian Misuse of Galatians 3:28

The primary weapon used to attack this distinction is Galatians 3:28: "There is neither Jew nor Greek, slave nor free, male nor female, for you are all one in Christ Jesus."

Critics argue this verse abolishes the "curse" of hierarchy. They claim that in the New Covenant, roles are erased. However, we must let Scripture interpret Scripture.

The "Slave nor Free" Parallel

Paul states there is "neither slave nor free" in Christ. Yet, in Ephesians 6:5, the same apostle commands: "Slaves, obey your earthly masters with respect and fear."

If Galatians 3:28 abolished social hierarchy, Paul's command in Ephesians 6 would be a contradiction. The slave is spiritually equal to the master (soteriological equality) but remains positionally subject to the master (functional subordination). Philemon 1:16 beautifully captures this tension, describing Onesimus as "no longer as a slave, but better than a slave, as a beloved brother." He is a brother in Christ, yet he is sent back to his master.

As mentioned in Chapter 2.2 refuting egalitarianism, Colossians 3:11 provides a strong witness: "Here there is no Gentile or Jew, circumcised or uncircumcised, barbarian, Scythian, slave or free, but Christ is all and is in all." Identical language, yet no one claims Colossians 3:11 abolishes the master-slave distinction in the household (see Col 3:22-4:1, where slaves are commanded to obey masters and masters to treat slaves justly). The spiritual equality in Christ (no distinction in standing before God) coexists with the functional distinctions God established in creation.

The "Male nor Female" Parallel

The same logic applies to the sexes. Galatians 3:28 declares that men and women have equal access to salvation. 1 Peter 3:7 states: "Husbands, in the same way, treat your wives with consideration as a delicate vessel, and with honor as fellow heirs of the gracious gift of life, so that your prayers will not be hindered." Peter calls the wife "the delicate vessel" (Greek: *asthenesterō skeuei*), acknowledging a positional distinction in strength and role. Yet he immediately describes her as a "fellow heir" (*synklēronomois*) of the gift of life. The same verse holds both truths: the wife is delicate in vessel (positional/functional), yet equal in inheritance (ontological/soteriological). This is the exact balance the chapter defends, no ontological inferiority, yet clear positional hierarchy. But this spiritual equality does not remove the created order of headship. Just as the gospel did not overthrow the master's authority in the home, it does not overthrow the husband's authority in the home or the elder's authority in the church.

The order is not arbitrary. 1 Corinthians 11:7-9 confirms: "A man ought not to cover his head, since he is the image and glory of God; but the woman is the glory of man. For man did not come from woman, but woman from man. Neither was man created for woman, but woman for man." Man is the glory of God, woman the glory of man. This is not ontological ranking (both are image-bearers per Gen 1:27), but a creational reflection of order: woman glorifies man by fulfilling her role under his headship, just as man glorifies God by fulfilling his.

The Consequence of Error

If we fail to maintain this distinction, we fall into one of two ditches.

- **The Error of Oppression:** If we deny ontological equality, we treat women as lesser beings or as mere property. This is a sin against the Creator who stamped His image upon them.
- **The Error of Rebellion:** If we deny positional subordination, we incite women to usurp the authority God delegated to men. This disrupts the divine order and invites judgment.

Occupy and Uphold

We must be mature enough to hold two truths at once. A woman is a co-heir of the Kingdom, fully equal in worth. A woman is also a subordinate helper, distinct in rank. To submit to a husband is not to admit inferiority. It is to occupy a station appointed by God for the good of the whole. Let us honor the value of the woman while upholding the authority of the man. This balance (positional subordination, ontological equality) flows from the Father's Chain of Headship: the Son submits to the Father without losing divine essence, so the woman submits to the man without losing image-bearing equality.

Reflection Questions

1. How does the parallel of "slave nor free" in Galatians 3:28 help explain why "male nor female" does not abolish male/female roles?
2. Why is it dangerous to conflate "rank" (position) with "value" (ontology)?
3. How does 1 Peter 3:7 affirm both the hierarchy ("delicate vessel") and the equality ("fellow heirs") of the woman?

> ***On Standing vs. State:*** *In the court of heaven, men and women stand side-by-side as children of God. In the household of earth, they stand face-to-face as head and helper. Both are true.*
>
> ***On Value:*** *Submission is not a statement of value. Jesus submits to the Father, yet He is God. If submission meant lesser value, the Trinity would collapse.*

PART II: THE INTERRUPTION (THE FALL)

Chapter 4: The Fall - From Harmony to Conflict

4.1 - Pre-Fall Harmony

Perfect Order Before Inversion Hierarchy is not a consequence of the Fall; it is the prerequisite for Paradise. God established the man as the head through the order of creation and the delivery of the moral law before the woman existed. Adam's failure was not a failure of instruction, as Eve knew the command, but a failure to maintain the divine order by listening to the voice of his wife rather than the voice of God.

🕮 THE WITNESSES

I. **Genesis 2**
16-17: "And the Lord God commanded him, 'You may eat freely from every tree of the garden, but you must not eat from the tree of the knowledge of good and evil; for in the day that you eat of it, you will surely die.'"

II. **Genesis 2**
18: "The LORD God also said, 'It is not good for the man to be alone. I will make for him a suitable helper.'"

III. **Genesis 3**
17: "And to Adam He said: 'Because you have listened to the voice of your wife and have eaten from the tree of which I commanded you not to eat, cursed is the ground because of you; through toil you will eat of it all the days of your life.'"

Harmony in Eden's Order

A pervasive error in modern theology suggests that authority and submission are consequences of the Curse. This view claims that in the Garden, Adam and Eve ruled as undifferentiated equals, and only after sin did God place the man in charge. Scripture explicitly refutes this timeline. The narrative of Genesis 2 provides irrefutable context that a vertical order was essential to the "very good" design of creation.

The Burden of the Law

Observe the sequence of events. God places the man in the Garden and issues the prohibition regarding the tree. At this moment, **the woman does not yet exist.**

"And the LORD God commanded him... you must not eat from the tree of the knowledge of good and evil" (Genesis 2:16-17).

God vests the authority of the Moral Law in Adam alone. He is held responsible for the instruction and protection of the sanctuary before Eve is formed. This establishes Adam as the **Federal Head**: the one liable for the obedience of his household. The woman enters into a world where the law has already been given to the man; she receives it through him, confirming his role as her head and teacher. We know Adam successfully communicated this law because Eve is able to quote it to the serpent in Genesis 3:2-3.

The Nature of the Tree and Adam's State

We must look closely at the specific name of the forbidden fruit: **"the tree of the knowledge of good and evil"** (Genesis 2:17).

This detail is critical for understanding the nature of the Fall. Prior to eating the fruit, Adam and Eve existed in a state of innocence. They did not possess the "knowledge of good and evil." This is confirmed in Genesis 3:22, where God states *after* the transgression: "Behold, the man has become like one of Us, knowing good and evil."

This changes how we view Adam's failure. He was not designed to navigate the Garden by moral intuition regarding evil, but by **obedience to the command of God.** Adam's test was not a test of moral reasoning; it was a test of hierarchy. He had the direct word of God ("do not eat"). When the moment of crisis came, he was faced with a choice of authority: The Voice of God or the action of his wife.

The Failure of "Listening"

Adam was with Eve when she ate (Genesis 3:6), yet he joined her in the transgression. While he was not deceived (1 Timothy 2:14), he followed her lead. The specific indictment God brings against Adam in Genesis 3:17 is telling: "Because you have listened to the voice of your wife and have eaten from the tree of which I commanded you not to eat..."

God does not indict Adam for failing to teach her; she knew the command. He indicts Adam for **inverting the order**. Adam placed the voice of the derivative (the woman) above the voice of the Source (God).

Therefore, hierarchy was the mechanism of safety. Had Adam exercised his headship and rejected the fruit based on God's command, the Fall would not have occurred. His sin was abdicating his station as head to follow his helper.

The Purpose of the Woman

The pre-Fall hierarchy is further cemented by the woman's design. "I will make for him a suitable helper" (Genesis 2:18).

The Hebrew *ezer* (helper) corresponds to him (*neged*). While she is his ontological equal, her function is defined by *his* need. She was created *for* the man (1 Corinthians 11:9), validating the directional flow of authority. Eve had agency; she was not a passive object. She made a choice to eat. But Adam's sin was that he allowed her agency to overrule the divine command entrusted to him.

The Results are In

Hierarchy is not the result of sin; it is the structure of harmony. The Fall was an inversion of this structure: the man listening to the woman, and the woman listening to the serpent, rather than all submitting to God. To reject biblical hierarchy today is to repeat the error of Eden. We must return to the order where the man obeys God, and the home follows the man's obedience.

Reflection Questions

1. How does the fact that God gave the law to Adam *before* Eve was created (Genesis 2:16-17) establish his role as Federal Head?
2. If Adam did not "know good and evil" before eating the fruit (Genesis 3:22), why is his sin defined as disobedience rather than ignorance?
3. How does Genesis 3:17 ("Because you have listened to the voice of your wife") confirm that the core issue of the Fall was an inversion of authority?

> ***On the Tree:*** *The tree was the test of authority. Adam could not know "evil" by experience or intuition yet. He could only know "duty" by the command of God. His failure was abandoning duty for solidarity with his wife.*
>
> ***On Listening:*** *The first sin of the man was listening to the wrong voice. Hierarchy is the discipline of tuning one's ear to the Source (God) rather than the derivative (the wife) when their wills conflict.*

4.2 - Post-Fall Consequences

Strife from Inversion (Teshuqah and Mashal) The Fall was a catastrophic breakdown of God's hierarchical design defined by a reversal of the flow of authority. The woman acted independently of her head, rejecting the word of God mediated through him. The man committed treason against his Head by listening to the voice of his wife over the direct command of God. While Christ provides the only remedy for the *guilt* of sin, the restoration of the *functional order* (God → Man → Woman) is the specific remedy for the domestic chaos unleashed by the Fall.

🕮 THE WITNESSES

I. **Genesis 3**
16: "To the woman He said: 'I will sharply increase your pain in childbirth; in pain you will bring forth children. Your desire will be for your husband, and he will rule over you.'"

II. **Genesis 3**
17: "And to Adam He said: 'Because you have listened to the voice of your wife and have eaten from the tree of which I commanded you not to eat, cursed is the ground because of you; through toil you will eat of it all the days of your life.'"

III. **Genesis 3**
2-3: "The woman answered the serpent, 'We may eat the fruit of the trees of the garden, but about the fruit of the tree in the middle of the garden, God has said, "You must not eat of it or touch it, or you will die."'"

The Crisis of Mediated Authority

To understand the mechanics of the Fall, we must recognize the specific position of the woman regarding the law. As established in **Chapter 4.1**, Adam received the prohibition directly from God before the woman was formed (Genesis 2:16-17). The woman did not hear the voice of God thunder this command; she received it through the teaching of her husband.

This places Eve in a position of **mediated authority**. Her obedience to God was inextricably linked to her trust in the word delivered by Adam. In Genesis 3:2-3, she quotes the command *almost* verbatim to the serpent (she added, "or touch it"), proving she had been taught. However, when the serpent challenged that word, she faced a test of hierarchy: Would she trust the instruction of her head, or would she act as an independent moral agent and trust the voice of another?

By taking the fruit, Eve did not merely break a rule; she bypassed the chain of command. She acted autonomously, judging the fruit "good for food" and "pleasing to the eyes" (Genesis 3:6) based on her own assessment, rejecting the covering of her husband's instruction and following the voice of a liar.

The Treason of the Man

Adam's failure was the precise inverse of Eve's. He possessed the direct revelation from God. He knew the command first-hand. Yet, Genesis 3:6 states she gave some to her husband "who was with her, and he ate it."

God's indictment in Genesis 3:17 pinpoints the exact nature of Adam's sin. It does not accuse him of being deceived, nor of him failing to "protect" Eve, nor does it accuse him of "blaming" her or God. The indictment is structural: "Because you have listened to the voice of your wife and have eaten..."

Adam's sin was **submitting to the wrong voice**. In the hierarchy of creation, the flow of authority is **God → Man →**

Woman. When Adam accepted the fruit from Eve, he inverted this flow. He placed the voice of the subordinate (his wife) above the voice of the Superior (God). He did not merely "stand by" in ignorance; he actively chose to follow her lead. He submitted to his wife rather than ruling his house in the fear of God. This was an act of high treason against the divine order. Even if a wife speaks truth, a husband must obey God directly, not the woman. To obey the woman is to invert the structure; to obey God is to uphold it.

The Result: Teshuqah and Mashal

The consequence of this inversion is the introduction of conflict into the male/female dynamic. God describes the new reality of the fallen household in Genesis 3:16: "Your desire will be for your husband, and he will rule over you."

The Desire (Teshuqah)

The Hebrew word *teshuqah* is often romanticized, but Scripture defines its meaning in the very next chapter. In Genesis 4:7, God warns Cain regarding sin: "it desires to have you, but you must master it."

In Genesis 4:7, *teshuqah* refers to a desire to possess, control, and usurp. Therefore, the curse upon the woman is not that she will long for her husband's affection, but that she will possess an innate, sinful drive to master him. The fall converted her calling as a "helper" into a competitor. She now desires to take the reins, mirroring her action in the garden where she took the initiative.

The Rule (Mashal)

God's response to this conflict is to reaffirm the hierarchy: "and he will rule over you." The Hebrew *mashal* indicates dominion and governance. Even in a fallen world, the man remains the head. However, because of the woman's desire to usurp (*teshuqah*), his rule often becomes a struggle. What was once a harmonious headship in Eden often degrades into a battle of wills, where the man must enforce authority or abdicate it entirely.

Order Required

The Fall was an act of anarchy against God's order. While the death and resurrection of Jesus Christ is the only remedy for the *guilt* of sin, the specific remedy for the *chaos* of the home is a return to God's hierarchical design. The woman must resist the urge to control (*teshuqah*) and learn to submit to the authority God placed over her. The man must repent of "listening to the voice of his wife" over the voice of God and resume his station as the head who obeys God first.

Reflection Questions

1. How does the fact that Adam received the law *before* Eve establish his role as the teacher and her role as the receiver of mediated authority?
2. Why is God's indictment "Because you have listened to the voice of your wife" (Genesis 3:17) critical for defining Adam's sin as an inversion of hierarchy?
3. How does the parallel between Genesis 3:16 and Genesis 4:7 define the "desire" of the woman as a struggle for control rather than romantic affection?

On Hierarchy: *The first sin was an inversion of the chain of headship. The woman acted as the head, and the man acted as the helper. Order is restored when the man submits to God and the woman submits to the man.*

On Leadership: *A husband must love his wife, but he must never submit to her authority. Even if her counsel is wise, he follows it because it aligns with God's will, not because she commanded it. To obey the wife is to repeat the error of Eden.*

PART III: SCRIPTURE'S UNIFIED WITNESS

Chapter 5: Old and New Testaments in Harmony

5.1 - Jesus Upholds the Law:

Creation Order Affirmed Jesus Christ, the Incarnate Word, affirms the immutability of the written Word, declaring that "the Scripture cannot be broken." He explicitly upholds the creation order of male and female "from the beginning" and rejects cultural concessions to sin. This high view of Scripture establishes the foundation for the New Testament's continuity with the Old, ensuring that the hierarchical commands found in the apostolic writings are viewed as unbreakable divine law, not temporary opinion.

🕮 THE WITNESSES

I. **Matthew 5**
 17-18: "Do not think that I have come to abolish the Law or the Prophets. I have not come to abolish them, but to fulfill them. For I tell you truly, until heaven and earth pass away, not a single jot, not a stroke of a pen, will disappear from the Law until everything is accomplished."

II. **Matthew 19**
 4: "Jesus answered, 'Have you not read that from the beginning the Creator "made them male and female,"'"

III. **John 10**
 35: "If he called them gods to whom the word of God came—and the Scripture cannot be broken—"

Christ Affirms Creation's Order

A common error in modern theology is the attempt to pit Jesus against Paul, or the New Testament against the Old. This argument suggests that while the Old Testament was patriarchal and hierarchical, Jesus came as a liberator to flatten all roles and establish a new egalitarian kingdom where distinction is abolished.

This view is directly refuted by the words of Christ Himself. Jesus did not come to dismantle the order of the Father; He came to restore it to its original intent.

The Immutability of Scripture (John 10:35)

Before we examine Jesus' specific teachings on men and women, we must establish His view of the Bible's authority. In John 10:35, while debating the Jewish leaders, Jesus makes a parenthetical statement that carries absolute theological weight: **"and the Scripture cannot be broken."**

The Greek word for "broken" here (*lythēnai*) means to be loosened, dissolved, or annulled. The *Logos* (the Living Word) declares that the *Graphe* (the Written Word) is indestructible. It cannot be set aside. It cannot be invalidated.

This has profound implications for our study of hierarchy. If Jesus declares that the Old Testament narrative is binding and unbreakable, then the creation order established in Genesis is binding and unbreakable. Furthermore, this sets the necessary precedent for the rest of the New Testament. As we will see in **Chapter 5.2**, the Apostle Peter classifies Paul's letters as "Scripture" (2 Peter 3:16). If Paul's letters are Scripture, and Jesus says Scripture "cannot be broken," then Paul's commands regarding the silence of women and the headship of men are unbreakable. To attempt to "break" them by calling them cultural is to defy the definition of Scripture given by Jesus Himself.

Fulfillment, Not Abolition (Matthew 5:17)

Jesus sets the standard for His ministry in the Sermon on the Mount: "Do not think that I have come to abolish the Law or the Prophets. I have not come to abolish them, but to fulfill them" (Matthew 5:17).

The Law established the priesthood, the structure of the family, and the distinction between the holy and the common. If Jesus had come to remove the headship of the man or the structure of authority, He would be abolishing the Law. Instead, He affirms that "not a single jot, not a stroke of a pen, will disappear from the Law" (Matthew 5:18).

We must understand what "fulfill" means in this context. It does not mean to make void; it means to fill to the fullest measure. Jesus fulfills the moral law by obeying it perfectly. He fulfills the ceremonial law by becoming the ultimate sacrifice. But He also fulfills the *social* law by modeling perfect submission to the Father and perfect headship over the Church. He validates the hierarchy established in Genesis.

The Appeal to "The Beginning" (Matthew 19:4)

When challenged by the Pharisees regarding divorce, Jesus does not appeal to current cultural trends or even to the Mosaic concessions found in Deuteronomy 24. He goes back to the absolute standard.

"Have you not read that from the beginning the Creator 'made them male and female,'" (Matthew 19:4).

By quoting Genesis 1:27 and Genesis 2:24, Jesus grounds His teaching in the **Creation Order**. He affirms that the design established before the Fall is the standard for the Kingdom. As we established in **Part II**, the pre-fall world was hierarchical. By pointing back to "the beginning," Jesus is not pointing to a future "evolved" state of sexless equality. He is pointing back to the Garden where the man was the head and the woman was the helper.

The Pharisees pointed out that Moses allowed divorce. Jesus clarifies the distinction between God's perfect will and a concession to sin: "Jesus replied, 'Moses permitted you to divorce your wives because of your hardness of heart; but it was not this way from the beginning.'" (Matthew 19:8).

This principle destroys the egalitarian argument. Egalitarians often argue that hierarchy is a result of the Fall (a concession to sin) and that Jesus brings us out of it. Jesus argues the exact opposite regarding the relationship of man and woman. The loose structure (easy divorce, relational chaos) is the concession to sin; the strict union and order of "the beginning" is the ideal.

The Model of Submission

Far from abolishing hierarchy, Jesus embodies it. He consistently affirms His submission to the Father. He states: "For I have come down from heaven, not to do My own will, but to do the will of Him who sent Me." (John 6:38).

If the Son of God submits to the Father without losing His divinity, then submission cannot be evil, degrading, or a consequence of the Fall. It is the very nature of the Godhead. By upholding the Law and submitting to the Father, Jesus validates the principle of authority and submission as eternal and good.

No Replacement Necessary

The New Testament does not replace the Order of Creation; it redeems it. Jesus calls us away from the "hardness of heart" that resents authority and back to the "beginning" where authority was exercised in love and submission was offered in trust. Most importantly, Jesus creates a sealed category called "Scripture" which He declares "cannot be broken." This prepares us to accept the hard sayings of the Apostles in the following chapters not as the opinions of men, but as the unbreakable law of God.

Reflection Questions

1. What is the significance of Jesus calling Scripture "unbreakable" (John 10:35) in relation to modern attempts to dismiss "difficult" passages about men and women?
2. How does Jesus' statement "it was not this way from the beginning" (Matthew 19:8) challenge the idea that society should "evolve" past biblical male/female roles?
3. If Jesus came to "fulfill" the Law (Matthew 5:17), can we legitimately claim that He abolished the structure of the family established in the Torah?

> ***On the Unbroken Word:*** *When culture demands we break the Scripture to fit the times, we must remember that the Rock of Ages said Scripture cannot be broken. We break ourselves against it if we try.*
>
> ***On The Beginning:*** *Every time Jesus defines marriage or the sexes, He quotes Genesis. If our theology of men and women contradicts Genesis, it contradicts Jesus.*

5.2 - Paul's Authority as Scripture

Affirmed by Witnesses Paul's divine apostleship and his letters are confirmed as authoritative Scripture (*graphe*) by multiple witnesses, specifically the Apostle Peter and the Lord Jesus Christ. Therefore, Paul's instructions regarding the hierarchy of man and woman are not the cultural opinions of a man but the unbreakable commandments of the Lord, carrying the full weight of the Old Testament canon.

🕮 THE WITNESSES

I. **2 Peter 3**
15-16: "Consider also that our Lord's patience brings salvation, just as our beloved brother Paul also wrote you with the wisdom God gave him. He writes this way in all his letters, speaking in them about such matters. Some parts of his letters are hard to understand, which ignorant and unstable people distort, as they do the rest of the Scriptures, to their own destruction."

II. **Acts 9**
15: "'Go!' said the Lord. 'This man is My chosen instrument to carry My name before the Gentiles and their kings, and before the people of Israel.'"

III. **Galatians 1**
11-12: "For I certify to you, brothers, that the gospel I preached was not devised by man. I did not receive it from any man, nor was I taught it; rather, I received it by revelation from Jesus Christ."

The Attack on the Apostle

In modern theological debates regarding male/female roles, a common tactic is to isolate the Apostle Paul. When faced with clear commands such as "I do not permit a woman to teach or to exercise authority over a man" (1 Timothy 2:12), critics often attempt to devalue these texts by contrasting them with the words of Jesus. They argue that Jesus was egalitarian while Paul was patriarchal, or that Paul's writings reflect his personal rabbinic biases rather than divine law.

To maintain the Forgotten Order, we must dismantle this division. If Paul's writings are Scripture, then they share the same authority as the words of Christ in the Gospels, for both proceed from the same Spirit.

Peter's Classification: "The Rest of the Scriptures"

The most powerful defense of Paul's authority comes from the Apostle Peter. In his final letter, Peter explicitly categorizes Paul's epistles as Scripture.

"He writes this way in all his letters... which ignorant and unstable people distort, as they do the **rest of the Scriptures**, to their own destruction" (2 Peter 3:16).

The phrase "the rest of the Scriptures" (*tas loipas graphas*) is exegetically decisive. Peter does not say "as they do the Scriptures," which might imply Paul's writing was something different. He says "the rest," placing Paul's letters in the exact same category as the Law, the Prophets, and the Psalms.

If Jesus declared that "the Scripture cannot be broken" (John 10:35), and Peter declares that Paul's writing is "Scripture," then Paul's writing cannot be broken. To dismiss Paul's commands on headship is to distort Scripture, an act Peter warns leads "to their own destruction."

The Source of Paul's Doctrine

Paul himself anticipates the charge that his teaching is merely human opinion. In Galatians 1, he provides a sworn affidavit regarding the source of his theology.

"I did not receive it from any man, nor was I taught it; rather, I received it by revelation from Jesus Christ" (Galatians 1:12).

Paul's understanding of the church, the home, and the order of creation was not derived from the Sanhedrin or even the other apostles. It was a direct revelation from the risen Lord. When Paul writes about the husband being the head of the wife (Ephesians 5:23), he is transmitting the will of Christ. To reject the messenger is to reject the King who sent him.

The Divine Commission

Luke, the historian of the early church, records the specific moment of Paul's commissioning. It was not a human appointment.

"'Go!' said the Lord. 'This man is My chosen instrument...'" (Acts 9:15).

Jesus calls Paul His "chosen instrument" (*skeuos eklogēs*). If we argue that Paul was wrong about male and female differences, we are arguing that Jesus chose a defective instrument to lay the foundation of the Church's social order. This attacks the sovereignty and wisdom of Christ. The validity of the New Testament hangs on the reliability of the apostles Jesus chose.

The Coherence of the Witnesses

We see a unified front:

1. **Jesus** chooses Paul as His voice to the Gentiles (Acts 9).
2. **Paul** claims his message comes directly from Jesus (Galatians 1).

3. **Peter** confirms Paul's writings are Scripture on par with the Old Testament (2 Peter 3).

Therefore, when we read 1 Corinthians 11 or 1 Timothy 2, we are not reading the "cultural musings of a first-century bachelor." We are reading the Word of God. The difficulty of these passages ("hard to understand," 2 Peter 3:16) is not an excuse to reject them. It is a warning to handle them with fear and trembling, lest we distort them to our own ruin.

No False Claims

The hierarchy of the home and church is not "Pauline theology" in contrast to "Christian theology." It is biblical theology. By establishing Paul's writings as Scripture, the Holy Spirit ensured that the Order of Creation would be codified as the Order of the Church. We cannot claim to follow Jesus while rejecting the Scriptures He inspired His chosen instrument to write.

However, because Paul's writings stand as the primary fortress of male/female distinction in the New Testament, he has become the primary target of modern critics. Since they cannot disprove the text, they attack the man. We must now turn our attention to these specific assaults on his character and commission, ensuring our foundation remains secure against those who would tear it down.

Reflection Questions

1. How does Peter's use of the phrase "the rest of the Scriptures" (2 Peter 3:16) change the way we must view Paul's letters?
2. If Paul received his gospel by "revelation from Jesus Christ" (Galatians 1:12), what are the implications of calling his teaching on the sexes "culturally obsolete"?
3. Why is it dangerous to separate the words of Jesus (in red letters) from the words of Paul (in black letters) when both are Scripture?

On Authority: *You cannot have a "Red Letter Christianity" that ignores the Epistles. The King (Jesus) speaks through His ambassadors (the Apostles). To ignore the ambassador is to insult the King.*

On Distortion: *Peter warns that twisting Paul's difficult words leads to destruction. This suggests that "egalitarian gymnastics," twisting texts to fit modern sensibilities, is a spiritually dangerous enterprise.*

5.3 - Addressing Common Attacks on Paul's Apostleship

The authority of the Apostle Paul is established not merely by his own claims but by the external testimony of the Lord Jesus Christ, the Apostle Peter, and the Jerusalem Council. To reject Paul's teaching on hierarchy is to reject the unified witness of the New Testament and the very Gospel writers who validated him. This accumulation of evidence is essential to satisfy the biblical requirement for establishing truth.

🕮 THE WITNESSES

I. **Acts 9**
 15: "'Go!' said the Lord. 'This man is My chosen instrument to carry My name before the Gentiles and their kings, and before the people of Israel.'"

II. **2 Peter 3**
 15-16: "Consider also that our Lord's patience brings salvation, just as our beloved brother Paul also wrote you with the wisdom God gave him. He writes this way in all his letters, speaking in them about such matters. Some parts of his letters are hard to understand, which ignorant and unstable people distort, as they do the rest of the Scriptures, to their own destruction."

III. **Acts 15**
 25-26: "So we all agreed to choose men to send to you along with our beloved Barnabas and Paul, men who have risked their lives for the name of our Lord Jesus Christ."

The Strategy of Divide and Conquer

A pervasive strategy in modern egalitarian theology is to drive a wedge between Jesus and Paul. Critics often suggest that while Jesus was inclusive and non-hierarchical, Paul hijacked the movement, reintroducing patriarchal structures from his own Jewish background or personal prejudices. They argue that Paul appointed himself and that his views on women should be categorized as personal opinion rather than divine law.

If we rely only on Paul's letters to defend Paul, the critic may claim circular reasoning. However, the New Testament provides a robust defense of Paul's authority through witnesses *other than Paul himself.* We must examine the testimony of the Historian (Luke), the Rock (Peter), and the Council (the Jerusalem leadership).

The Testimony of Luke (Acts 9)

The most critical witness to Paul's authority is the Lord Jesus Himself. This testimony is recorded by Luke in the book of Acts. We must remember that Luke is not merely a historian of the early church; he is a Gospel writer. The same man who recorded the birth of Jesus, the parable of the Prodigal Son, and the road to Emmaus also recorded the divine commissioning of Paul. To accuse Luke of falsifying Paul's authority in Acts is to undermine the reliability of the Gospel of Luke. We cannot have the Manger without the Road to Damascus.

In Acts 9, a disciple named Ananias is hesitant to approach Saul (Paul) due to his violent reputation. The Lord Jesus speaks directly to Ananias, validating Paul's role before Paul had written a single epistle.

""Go!" said the Lord. "This man is My chosen instrument to carry My name before the Gentiles and their kings, and before the people of Israel."" (Acts 9:15).

Paul did not volunteer; he was conscripted. Jesus calls him a "chosen instrument" (*skeuos eklogēs*). To reject Paul's teaching is to question the wisdom of the Carpenter who chose His own tool. If Paul's theology of the sexes is flawed, then Jesus chose a defective instrument to lay the foundation of the Church among the nations.

The Endorsement of Peter

Peter's endorsement of Paul's authority is decisive. In 2 Peter 3:15-16 he calls Paul "our beloved brother Paul" and places his letters on par with "the rest of the Scriptures."

This affirmation carries even greater force because it comes after Paul publicly opposed Peter to his face in Antioch for hypocrisy. Galatians 2:11-14 records the confrontation (*Cephas is Peter's Aramaic name*): "When Cephas came to Antioch, however, I opposed him to his face, because he stood to be condemned. For before certain men came from James, he used to eat with the Gentiles. But when they arrived, he began to draw back and separate himself, for fear of those in the circumcision group. The other Jews joined him in his hypocrisy, so that by their hypocrisy even Barnabas was led astray. When I saw that they were not walking in line with the truth of the gospel, I said to Cephas in front of them all, 'If you, who are a Jew, live like a Gentile and not like a Jew, how can you compel the Gentiles to live like Jews?'"

The rebuke was sharp and open. Yet Peter does not retaliate, reject Paul, or withdraw his support. In his later epistle he still names Paul "our beloved brother" and treats his writings as Scripture. This proves the correction was fraternal discipline within apostolic unity, not personal division or denial of Paul's divine commission. The same Peter who was rebuked publicly affirms Paul's letters as authoritative, confirming that the apostles spoke with one voice, even after confrontation.

The Consensus of the Council (Acts 15)

Finally, we have the corporate witness of the early church leadership. In Acts 15, the apostles and elders gathered to settle doctrinal disputes. If Paul were a rogue agent teaching false doctrine, this was the moment to silence him.

Instead, the Council sent a letter to the Gentile believers endorsing Paul's ministry without reservation. They wrote: "So we all agreed to choose men to send to you along with our beloved Barnabas and Paul, men who have risked their lives for the name of our Lord Jesus Christ" (Acts 15:25-26).

The leaders of the Jerusalem church called him "beloved" and recognized his sacrificial service for the name of Christ. There is no historical evidence of a division between the Twelve and Paul regarding his authority or his teaching.

The Chosen Instrument

The claim that Paul hijacked the faith is historically and theologically untenable. He was commissioned by Christ (Acts 9), endorsed by the Jerusalem Council (Acts 15), and canonized by Peter (2 Peter 3). When we read Paul's instructions on the headship of the husband or the silence of women in the church, we are reading the words of Christ's chosen instrument.

Why is this accumulation of evidence so important? It is because the Bible establishes a legal framework for truth. God does not ask us to blindly follow a solitary voice. He has established a standard of verification known as the "Principle of Witnesses." In the next chapter, we will see how this principle protects the doctrine of hierarchy from being dismissed as an isolated cultural artifact, proving that the order of the home and church is established by the unified testimony of the Law, the Prophets, and the Apostles.

Reflection Questions

1. How does rejecting Luke's account of Paul's conversion in Acts undermine our confidence in the Gospel of Luke?
2. Why is the "chosen instrument" designation by Jesus (Acts 9:15) vital for accepting Paul's difficult teachings on the sexes?
3. How does the endorsement of the Jerusalem Council (Acts 15) refute the modern idea that Paul was a rogue theologian?

> ***On Authority:*** *We do not follow Paul because we like his personality; we follow him because the King chose him. To reject the ambassador is to insult the King.*
>
> ***On Unity:*** *The Bible is not a collection of competing theologies. Peter, Paul, and Luke speak with one voice. The attempt to divide them is an attempt to escape their authority.*

5.4 - The Principle of Witnesses in Action

The doctrine of male headship and female submission is not the isolated opinion of the Apostle Paul but is a matter of divine law established by the unified testimony of three independent biblical witnesses: The Law (Moses), the Gospel (Jesus), and the Epistles (Paul).

🕮 THE WITNESSES

I. **Deuteronomy 19**
 15: "A lone witness is not sufficient to establish any wrongdoing or sin against a man, regardless of what offense he may have committed. A matter must be established by the testimony of two or three witnesses."

II. **Matthew 18**
 16: "But if he will not listen, take one or two others along, so that 'every matter may be established by the testimony of two or three witnesses.'"

III. **2 Corinthians 13**
 1: "This is the third time I am coming to you. 'Every matter must be established by the testimony of two or three witnesses.'"

The "Lone Witness" Objection

It is common in modern church culture to hear the argument that we should not build a major doctrine on "a few isolated verses." Critics of biblical hierarchy often argue that the commands for women to submit or for men to lead are found only in a few of Paul's letters, specifically 1 Timothy and 1 Corinthians. They suggest that these are "cultural outliers" that contradict the broader, inclusive spirit of the Bible. This argument appeals to our sense of fairness; it seems reasonable to assume that if a teaching is truly from God, it should be pervasive rather than hidden in the corners of a few epistles. If Paul is the "lone witness" to this hierarchy, the argument goes, perhaps we can dismiss his instructions as temporary local solutions rather than universal commands. This view offers comfort to those who wish to avoid conflict with modern egalitarian sensibilities.

The Biblical Standard of Evidence

However, God has not left us to determine truth by our feelings or by counting the votes of modern culture. He has provided a rigorous legal standard for establishing validity within His Kingdom. As defined in Deuteronomy 19:15 and reaffirmed by Jesus Himself in Matthew 18:16, "A matter must be established by the testimony of two or three witnesses." This principle is not merely for criminal trials; the Apostle Paul applies it to doctrinal and disciplinary matters in the church (2 Corinthians 13:1). Therefore, to determine if hierarchy is God's eternal will, we must call the witnesses to the stand. We will find that Paul does not stand alone. He is joined by the Law and the Lord Jesus Himself.

Calling the Witnesses

We must now apply the Law of Witnesses to the doctrine of male headship. Does the Bible provide the necessary two or three witnesses to establish this truth?

Witness 1: The Testimony of the Law (Moses) The first witness is Moses, the writer of the Torah. Long before Paul wrote to the Ephesians, the order was established in Eden.

- **Genesis 2:18:** "The LORD God also said, 'It is not good for the man to be alone. I will make for him a suitable helper.'" Moses establishes that the man was the source (*kephale*) and the woman was created *for* the man as his helper (*ezer*). This testimony confirms that hierarchy is embedded in the fabric of creation.

Witness 2: The Testimony of the Gospel (Jesus) The second witness is the Lord Jesus Christ. Critics often try to pit Jesus against Paul, claiming Jesus liberated women from hierarchy. Yet, when Jesus defines marriage and authority, He points back to the first witness.

- **Matthew 19:4:** "Jesus answered, 'Have you not read that from the beginning the Creator "made them male and female,"...?'" By citing "the beginning," Jesus validates the Genesis order. Furthermore, Jesus models this hierarchy within the Trinity.
- **John 6:38:** "For I have come down from heaven, not to do My own will, but the will of Him who sent Me." Jesus does not abolish the order of authority; He perfectly fulfills it through submission to the Father.

Witness 3: The Testimony of the Epistles (Paul) The third witness is the Apostle Paul, who codifies the testimony of Moses and Jesus for the church.

- **1 Corinthians 11:3:** "But I want you to understand that the head of every man is Christ, and the head of the woman is man, and the head of Christ is God." Paul's teaching is not an innovation. It is the necessary conclusion drawn from the first two witnesses. The three voices: Moses, Jesus, and Paul, speak in perfect unison.

Impeaching the Witnesses

A common distortion in the church today is the attempt to "impeach the witnesses." In a court of law, if the testimony is damaging and irrefutable, the opposing lawyer will try to discredit the witness himself. Modern theology does exactly this.

- They impeach **Moses** by claiming the Creation account is merely a myth or a reflection of an ancient patriarchal society, denying that it establishes a universal pattern.
- They impeach **Paul** by claiming he was a misogynist or that he was simply trying to keep the church from offending Roman culture.
- They attempt to neutralize **Jesus** by claiming He was silent on the issue, ignoring that He explicitly affirmed the Law and the Prophets (Matthew 5:17).

This is not exegesis; it is evasion. To dismiss the unified testimony of the Law, the Gospel, and the Epistles because it conflicts with modern values is to place oneself as the judge over Scripture. It is an attempt to silence the witnesses God has called.

The Verdict of Scripture

The verdict is in. The matter of male headship is "established" (Deuteronomy 19:15). It is not a cultural preference or a Pauline quirk. It is a divine decree witnessed by the Law, the Son, and the Spirit speaking through the apostles. We must therefore submit to this truth with confidence. Do not apologize for the order of your home or your church. When you uphold male headship, you are standing on the solid rock of Scripture's unified witness. To reject it is to stand against the Law, the Gospel, and the Epistles.

Reflection Questions

1. Why is the "Principle of Witnesses" (Deut 19:15) essential for protecting the church from false doctrine and subjective interpretations?
2. How does seeing the agreement between Moses (Gen 2), Jesus (Matt 19), and Paul (1 Cor 11) refute the idea that headship is only a "cultural" issue?

3. How does the modern tendency to dismiss biblical authors as "culturally conditioned" mirror the legal tactic of impeaching a witness to avoid their testimony?

> ***On Evidence:*** *"A doctrine built on one verse is a castle built on sand. A doctrine built on the unified testimony of the Law, the Prophets, and the Apostles is a fortress on a rock."*
>
> ***On Unity:*** *"The Bible does not stutter. When Moses, Jesus, and Paul all point in the same direction regarding the order of men and women, it is not a 'cultural suggestion.' It is a command."*

Chapter 6: Hierarchy Across the Canon - Genesis to Revelation

6.1 - Old Testament Patterns

Patriarchy, Priesthood, Prophecy The Old Testament establishes a unified testimony of male headship through the rule of the husband (patriarchy) and the exclusive male priesthood, while distinguishing prophecy as a separate category that does not confer governing authority.

🕮 THE WITNESSES

I. **Genesis 3**
16: "To the woman He said: 'I will sharply increase your pain in childbirth; in pain you will bring forth children. Your desire will be for your husband, and he will rule over you.'"

II. **Exodus 28**
1: "Next, have your brother Aaron brought to you from among the Israelites, along with his sons Nadab, Abihu, Eleazar, and Ithamar, to serve Me as priests."

III. **2 Kings 22**
14: "So Hilkiah the priest, Ahikam, Achbor, Shaphan, and Asaiah went and spoke to Huldah the prophetess, the wife of Shallum son of Tikvah, the son of Harhas, the keeper of the wardrobe. She lived in Jerusalem, in the Second District."

The "Cultural Accommodation" Argument

It is widely taught today that the male-dominated structures of the Old Testament were merely a reflection of the primitive, patriarchal cultures of the ancient Near East. Critics argue that God simply accommodated the sexism of the times rather than endorsing it as an ideal. They suggest that the "trajectory" of Scripture moves away from this "repressive" system toward a full egalitarianism where male/female distinctions in authority are erased. They point to women like Miriam, Deborah, and Huldah as evidence that God frequently bypassed His own male-centric system to empower women, thereby invalidating the "rule" of male headship. If God used women as prophets, they reason, He clearly does not intend to restrict leadership to men in the church or home today.

The Divine Statute

However, this view collapses when we examine the text closely. The male leadership found in Israel was not merely a cultural accident. It was a matter of specific, written divine law. God did not simply tolerate a male priesthood. He commanded it. In Exodus 28:1, God explicitly selected "Aaron... along with his sons" to serve as priests. This statute was never repealed throughout the entire history of Israel. Furthermore, God codified the rule of the husband in Genesis 3:16, stating, "he will rule over you." Therefore, the pattern of the Old Testament is not a cultural relic to be discarded. It is a divine blueprint that establishes the distinction between *office* (governance) and *gift* (prophecy). We must let the Law and the Prophets interpret themselves rather than imposing modern sociological theories upon them.

The Threefold Pattern

To understand the Old Testament witness on hierarchy, we must examine three distinct categories: The Rule of the House (Patriarchy), The Rule of the Sanctuary (Priesthood), and The Revelation of the Word (Prophecy).

Pattern 1: The Rule of the Husband (Patriarchy) The first witness is the domestic order. Following the Fall, God affirmed the man's position as the head of the wife.

- **Genesis 3:16:** "Your desire will be for your husband, and he will rule over you." The Hebrew word for "rule" (*mashal*) implies governance and dominion. This structure is foundational to the social organization of God's people. Throughout the Torah, the census and genealogy are reckoned by "the head of each family" (Numbers 1:4). The covenant sign of circumcision was given to males (Genesis 17:10). The inheritance of the land was passed through the sons unless there were none (Numbers 27:8-11). This patriarchy was not a result of sin. It was God's method for ordering society and preserving the covenant line.

Pattern 2: The Restriction of the Priesthood The second witness is the religious order. If hierarchy were merely cultural, we would expect God to allow women to serve as priests, as was common in the surrounding pagan cults of Egypt and Babylon. Yet, God established a strictly, male priesthood.

- **Exodus 28:1:** "Next, have your brother Aaron brought to you from among the Israelites, along with his sons Nadab, Abihu, Eleazar, and Ithamar, to serve Me as priests." Throughout the Levitical law, the duties of the altar, the offering of sacrifices, and the entering of the Holy Place were exclusive to men (Leviticus 1:5). No woman ever served as a priest in Israel. This exclusion was not due to a lack of spiritual capability in women. It was due to the design of *representation*. The priest represented the people before God, a role of federal headship that belongs to the man. To violate this order was to invite judgment (Numbers 16).

Pattern 3: The Distinction of Prophecy The third witness clarifies the nature of exceptions. Critics cite prophetesses like Miriam (Exodus 15:20) and Huldah (2 Kings 22:14) to argue against male headship. However, we must distinguish between *prophecy* (receiving a message) and *office* (holding governing authority).

- **2 Kings 22:14:** "So Hilkiah the priest, Ahikam, Achbor, Shaphan, and Asaiah went and spoke to Huldah the prophetess, the wife of Shallum son of Tikvah, the son of Harhas, the keeper of the wardrobe. She lived in Jerusalem, in the Second District." God indeed spoke through Huldah. Yet, observe the structure. She was under the covering of her husband Shallum. She did not go to the temple to officiate. She did not sit on the throne to rule. The leaders came to her private residence to inquire of God. The governance of the nation remained with the King (Josiah), and the governance of the temple remained with the Priest (Hilkiah). Her role confirms that while women may receive and speak God's word, this gift does not overturn the order of male headship in the home or the sanctuary. The spirit of prophecy does not negate the law of priesthood.

The Prophetic Distinction

To understand the Old Testament witness, we must distinguish between *prophecy* (a charismatic gift) and *priesthood* (a statutory office).

We have already established in **Chapter 2.2** that the rise of female governance often serves as a divine indictment against male abdication, a sign that "women rule over them" (Isaiah 3:12). However, here we must observe the structural boundaries God preserved even during such exceptions. While God used women like Miriam (Exodus 15:20) and Deborah (Judges 4:4) as prophetesses, He never appointed them to the priesthood.

The Limit of the Exception Deborah was under the covering of her husband Lappidoth. Deborah judged Israel, yet she did not offer sacrifices. She spoke the word of God, but she did not officiate at the altar. The priesthood was exclusively male, restricted by divine statute to "Aaron... and his sons" (Exodus 28:1). This distinction is vital. Prophecy is a *gift* of the Spirit that God may distribute as He wills, but the Priesthood and the Headship of the

Fathers' Houses are *offices* of authority established by Law. The presence of a female prophetess does not overturn the male requirement for the office of oversight. To confuse the *gift* of revelation with the *office* of governance is a fundamental error in ecclesiology.

Order in the House of God

The Old Testament witness is unified. God establishes order through male headship in the family and male leadership in the assembly. This pattern is not accidental. It reflects the unchanging nature of God's design. Today, we must uphold this distinction. We celebrate the gifts of women who, like Huldah, speak truth and share wisdom. Yet, we maintain the order of the "fathers' houses" and the "priesthood" by reserving the office of elder and pastor for qualified men. By doing so, we do not devalue women. We honor the structure God created for the harmony and holiness of His people.

Reflection Questions

1. How does the restriction of the Levitical priesthood to "Aaron... and his sons" (Exodus 28:1) challenge the idea that male leadership was just a cultural accident?
2. Why is it important to distinguish between the *gift* of prophecy (which women exercised) and the *office* of priesthood (which was restricted to men)?
3. How does Isaiah 3:12 help us interpret the rise of female rulers as a sign of judgment rather than an ideal to be pursued?

> ***On Priesthood:*** *"God could have chosen women priests if He wanted to reflect the culture of Egypt or Canaan. Instead, He established a male-only priesthood to reflect His own Fatherhood and the order of creation."*
>
> ***On Exceptions:*** *"Exceptions like Deborah do not disprove the rule. They prove the rule is broken. When men fail to lead, the rise of female leadership is not a liberation. It is a judgment."*

6.2 - Prophecy vs. Teaching

The Apostolic Distinction Prophecy is Spirit-led edification under authority and is permitted to women, while authoritative teaching of doctrine over men is strictly forbidden to women by apostolic command rooted in creation.

🕮 THE WITNESSES

I. **1 Timothy 2**
12: "I do not permit a woman to teach or to exercise authority over a man; she is to remain quiet."

II. **1 Corinthians 14**
34: "Women are to be silent in the churches. They are not permitted to speak, but must be in submission, as the law says."

III. **1 Corinthians 11**
5: "And every woman who prays or prophesies with her head uncovered dishonors her head, for it is just as if her head were shaved."

The Confusion of Gifts and Office

A primary strategy of egalitarian theology is to conflate the gift of prophecy with the office of teaching. The argument is often presented in this manner: Since women like Miriam, Huldah, and the daughters of Philip prophesied in Scripture, and since prophecy involves speaking to the people, then women must be permitted to preach, teach, and hold authority in the church today. If the Spirit speaks through women, they reason, who are we to silence them? This argument appeals to our desire not to "quench the Spirit."

However, it fails to recognize the biblical distinction between *prophecy*, which is immediate edification, and *teaching*, which is the authoritative transmission of doctrine. By blurring these lines, modern theology creates a contradiction where none exists in the text.

Defining the Apostolic Distinction

The Apostles did not view prophecy and teaching as identical functions. Paul, writing under the inspiration of the Holy Spirit, establishes clear boundaries for both. He permits women to pray and prophesy (1 Corinthians 11:5) provided they maintain the symbol of authority. Yet he explicitly forbids them to teach or exercise authority over men (1 Timothy 2:12). This is not a contradiction. It is a distinction of function. Prophecy is addressed to men for "edification, encouragement, and comfort" (1 Corinthians 14:3). In contrast, teaching (*didaskein*) involves the authoritative definition and preservation of doctrine. The Spirit may move a woman to share a word of encouragement or insight, but the Spirit does not contradict His own command regarding the structure of authority in the household of God.

The Prohibition of Authority

We must first understand the restriction placed on the office of teaching. In 1 Timothy 2:12, Paul writes, "I do not permit a woman to teach or to exercise authority over a man; she is to remain quiet." Paul links "teaching" directly with "exercising authority" (*authentein*). In the context of the pastoral epistles, teaching is the primary function of the overseer. It is the act of establishing doctrine and correcting error. Paul forbids this role to women. He does not do this because they are incapable, but because it violates the created order. He grounds this prohibition immediately in Genesis: "For Adam was formed first, then Eve" (1 Timothy 2:13). The restriction is not cultural. It is creational.

The Regulation of Order

While teaching is forbidden, speech in the assembly is regulated by the principle of submission. In 1 Corinthians 14:34, the command is explicit: "Women are to be silent in the churches. They are not permitted to speak, but must be in submission, as the law says." This command appears in the context of "weighing" or judging prophecies. While women may prophesy, the authoritative evaluation of that prophecy, determining if it aligns with the faith, is a function of headship. In this authoritative context, women are to remain silent and in submission. Their silence is a sign of their subjection to the male leadership of the church. This ensures that the order of the Law is upheld even during charismatic expressions.

The Sign of Submission

The distinction is further clarified by the regulations on how a woman is to prophesy. In 1 Corinthians 11:5, Paul writes, "And every woman who prays or prophesies with her head uncovered dishonors her head, for it is just as if her head were shaved." Here, Scripture acknowledges that women *do* prophesy. If they were absolutely forbidden to speak a word under any circumstance, the regulating of their appearance while speaking would be unnecessary. However, the condition is critical: she must have her head covered. This physical symbol testifies that while she is speaking a word from God, she remains under the authority of her head (man). She is not overturning the hierarchy. She is operating within it.

The Danger of Conflation

When the church conflates prophecy and teaching, it inevitably erodes male headship. If a woman's subjective impression from the Spirit is given the same weight as the authoritative exposition of Scripture, she effectively becomes a leader over men. This opens the door to emotionalism and doctrinal drift. The objective standard of the Word (taught by qualified men) is replaced by the subjective experiences of the congregation. The Apostles maintained a rigid wall between the *gift* that edifies and the *office* that governs. To tear down this wall is to invite disorder and to disobey the plain command of Scripture.

Order in the Assembly

The New Testament continuity is clear: God desires both the vibrant working of the Spirit and the stable order of authority. Women are free to exercise their spiritual gifts, including prophecy, within the boundaries God has set. They may pray, and they may share words of edification. But the pulpit, the place of authoritative teaching and governance, is reserved for men. This is not to silence women but to protect the church. By maintaining this apostolic distinction, we honor the design of the Creator and ensure that the church remains the pillar and foundation of the truth.

Reflection Questions

1. How does the definition of prophecy in 1 Corinthians 14:3 ("edification, encouragement, and comfort") differ from the authority implied in "teaching" (1 Timothy 2:12)?
2. Why does Paul appeal to the formation of Adam and Eve (Creation) rather than the culture of Ephesus to support the restriction on teaching?
3. How does the requirement of a head covering in 1 Corinthians 11 reinforce the principle that spiritual gifts do not nullify male/female hierarchy?

> ***On Gifts vs. Office:*** *"A woman may have a gift of speaking, but she does not have the office of teaching. The Spirit distributes gifts, but the Word establishes order. We must not use the Spirit to disobey the Word."*
>
> ***On Silence:*** *"The silence of women in the church is not a silence of value, but a silence of governance. It is the silence of a soldier standing at attention while the officers confer."*

6.3 - New Testament Continuity

Christ → Church → Home The order of the home mirrors the order of the Godhead. Just as Christ submits to the Father without loss of value, the wife submits to the husband. This establishes a seamless continuity of authority flowing from God to Christ, from Christ to Man, and from Man to Woman.

THE WITNESSES

I. **1 Corinthians 11**
   3: "But I want you to understand that the head of every man is Christ, and the head of the woman is man, and the head of Christ is God."
II. **John 6**
   38: "For I have come down from heaven, not to do My own will, but the will of Him who sent Me."
III. **Ephesians 5**
   23: "For the husband is the head of the wife as Christ is the head of the church, His body, of which He is the Savior."

The Seamless Fabric of Divine Order

Modern critics often argue that submission implies inferiority. They claim that if a wife must submit to her husband, she must be of lesser value than him. This argument fails because it ignores the supreme model of authority found in the Trinity itself. The New Testament does not present the hierarchy of the home as a result of the Fall or a cultural relic. It presents it as a reflection of the eternal relationship between God the Father and God the Son. To reject the concept of functional subordination, where one equal person submits to another equal person, is to reject the nature of Christ's relationship with the Father. The order of the home is natural because it is supernatural. It is designed to image the forgotten order of the Godhead.

The Trinitarian Archetype

The first witness establishes the universal chain of command. In 1 Corinthians 11:3, Paul writes, "But I want you to understand that the head of every man is Christ, and the head of the woman is man, and the head of Christ is God." This verse is the theological anchor for all male/female roles. We must observe the sequence carefully. The woman is under the headship of the man. Is this degradation? It is no more degradation than Christ being under the headship of God the Father.

This text refutes the egalitarian claim that authority requires inequality. Christ is equal to the Father in essence. As He declares in John 10:30, "I and the Father are one." Yet He is subordinate in role and function. He submits to the headship of the Father. Therefore, submission cannot mean inferiority. If Christ can submit to the Father while maintaining His divinity and worth, the wife can submit to the husband while maintaining her full equality as an image-bearer. The hierarchy of the home is a picture of the hierarchy of heaven.

The Reality of Submission in the Godhead

The second witness proves that this submission within the Godhead is active and functional. Jesus declares in John 6:38, "For I have come down from heaven, not to do My own will, but the will of Him who sent Me." Christ, though fully God, takes the posture of a servant. He does not seek His own agenda but aligns perfectly with the authority of the Father. This divine patriarchy is the structure of the universe. The Father leads. The Son submits and executes.

This does not decrease the Son's value. Instead, it manifests His glory.

When a husband leads his home and a wife submits to him, they are reenacting this divine dynamic. The husband represents the Father's authoritative love. The wife represents the Son's willing support and glory. To despise submission is to despise the spirit of Christ. To reject headship is to reject the position of the Father.

The Application to Marriage

The third witness brings this theology down to the practical level of marriage. Ephesians 5:23 states, "For the husband is the head of the wife as Christ is the head of the church, His body, of which He is the Savior." The husband's headship is not a license for tyranny. It is also not a position he earned by merit. It is a functional office assigned by God to reflect Christ.

The wife's submission is not a reflection of weakness. It is a reflection of the Church's relationship to Christ, and ultimately, Christ's relationship to the Father. To dismantle the rule of the father in the home is to obscure the picture of the rule of God over creation. The home is the training ground where we learn to respect the principle of headship that governs all of reality.

The Danger of Disconnecting the Chain

We must understand the stakes. If we argue that the headship of the man is merely cultural, we risk implying that the headship of God over Christ is merely cultural or temporary. The Apostle Paul links them in an unbreakable chain in 1 Corinthians 11:3. We cannot break the link between man and woman without shattering the logic that connects Christ to God. By upholding the hierarchy of the home, we uphold the doctrine of the Trinity. By rejecting it, we invite a theology that eventually denies the distinctions within the Godhead itself.

The Natural Flow

The continuity is absolute. God the Father is the Head of Christ. Christ is the Head of the man. The man is the head of the woman. This is the natural flow of authority. It flows from the uncreated Godhead into the created order of the family. When we embrace this, we do not merely follow a cultural tradition. We participate in a divine pattern. We uphold the truth that role distinction does not destroy essential equality, a truth proved by the Father and the Son.

This biblical testimony is unbroken. We have seen from the beginning of Genesis to the writings of the Apostles that the vertical order of Creation is God's design. However, a competing narrative has arisen in our time, claiming that this order is an archaic form of oppression that the church must outgrow. To confront this error, we must now turn our eyes from the changeless Word of God to the changing tides of human history. We will discover that the rejection of this order is a modern anomaly, a deviation from the path walked by the faithful for nearly two thousand years.

Reflection Questions

1. How does the truth that "the head of Christ is God" (1 Corinthians 11:3) refute the modern idea that submission implies inferiority?
2. If Christ came "not to do My own will" (John 6:38), what does this teach us about the dignity and holiness of submission within the family?
3. How does viewing the father's leadership in the home as a reflection of God the Father's rule change the way we approach family discipline and order?

> ***On Submission:*** *"Submission is not a sign of weakness. It is the posture of the Son of God. To submit is to be like Jesus."*
>
> ***On Headship:*** *"Headship is not about privilege. It is about responsibility. The husband bears the weight of the home just as Christ bears the weight of the Church."*

PART IV: HISTORICAL ECHOES AND EARLY CHURCH WITNESS

Chapter 7: Historical Echoes - Inversions, Insights, and Apostolic Continuity

7.1 - Feminist Errors in Context

From Suffrage to Complementarianism The historical progression from the suffrage movement to modern feminism represents a calculated rebellion against the created order, while the church's response of "Complementarianism" has often compromised biblical patriarchy in an attempt to accommodate cultural shifts.

🕮 THE WITNESSES

I. **Isaiah 3**
12: "Youths oppress My people, and women rule over them. O My people, your guides mislead you; they turn you from your paths."

II. **Titus 2**
5: "to be self-controlled, pure, managers of their households, kind, and submissive to their own husbands, so that the word of God will not be discredited."

III. **Genesis 3**
16: "To the woman He said: 'I will sharply increase your pain in childbirth; in pain you will bring forth children. Your desire will be for your husband, and he will rule over you.'"

The Plea for Justice

It is important to acknowledge that the feminist movement did not arise in a vacuum. Throughout history, sinful men have abused their authority, failing to love their wives as Christ loved the church.

In the 19th and early 20th centuries, many women faced genuine hardships. They lacked legal protections[1], were vulnerable to the vices of alcoholic husbands, and often had no recourse against abuse. The early calls for suffrage and women's rights were framed as a moral necessity to protect the home and the dignity of women[2]. To the modern mind, opposing these movements seems like an endorsement of tyranny. It is natural to feel that giving women a voice in the public square was the only way to correct the failures of men.

The Nature of the Remedy

However, we must distinguish between the reality of the grievance and the nature of the remedy. While the grievance of abuse was real, the remedy of dismantling the household order was unbiblical. God's solution to the failure of men is not the empowerment of women to rule, but the repentance of men to rule well. The trajectory of feminism was not merely about protection. It was about power. It was the collective manifestation of the curse found in Genesis 3:16, where God stated, "Your desire will be for your husband, and he will rule over you." This desire is not romantic. It is a desire to master and control. History shows us that when the structure of authority is broken to solve a problem, the result is not justice but anarchy.

The Historical Progression

We can trace this rebellion through three distinct phases, each moving further from the biblical pattern established in Creation.

---

[1] Blackstone defines the concept of **coverture**, where a woman's legal rights were subsumed by those of her husband upon marriage. This is the legal reality early feminists were reacting against - Blackstone, William. *Commentaries on the Laws of England*. Vol. 1. Oxford: Clarendon Press, 1765. (specifically Chapter 15, "Of Husband and Wife").

[2] The WCTU was the largest women's organization in the 19th century and argued for the vote primarily to protect the home from the effects of alcohol abuse (the "Home Protection" ballot). - Willard, Frances. *Woman and Temperance: Or, The Work and Workers of the Woman's Christian Temperance Union*. Hartford: Park Publishing Co., 1883

Phase 1: The Political usurpation (Suffrage) The demand for the vote was a fundamental shift from the family as the basic unit of society to the individual[3]. Biblically, the husband represents the household. When the vote was granted to individuals rather than households, it split the political voice of the family and undermined the headship of the father. It was the first step in declaring that a woman's interests were separate from, and potentially opposed to, her husband's.

Phase 2: The Domestic Rebellion Following political independence came the rejection of the domestic sphere. The "Second Wave" of feminism explicitly attacked the role of the homemaker and female identity[4]. Yet the Bible is clear regarding the woman's domain. In Titus 2:5, Paul commands young women "to be self-controlled, pure, managers of their households, kind, and submissive to their own husbands." The Greek term *oikourgos* (managers of households) defines her primary sphere of influence. Feminism labeled this slavery[5]. Scripture calls it high calling.

Phase 3: The Erasure of Distinction The final phase, which we are living in today, is the total erasure of male/female distinctions. If authority is arbitrary and roles are interchangeable, then sexual identity itself becomes a social construct[6]. This is the logical conclusion of rejecting the order of Genesis.

---

[3] Bushnell, Horace. *Women's Suffrage: The Reform Against Nature*. New York: Charles Scribner, 1869. Beecher, Catherine. *Woman's Suffrage and Woman's Profession*. Hartford: Brown & Gross, 1871. (Both authors argued that the family, not the individual, was the state's political unit, and the man voted as the representative head of that unit.)

[4] Foundational text arguing that "One is not born, but rather becomes, a woman," separating biological sex from gender role. - de Beauvoir, Simone. *The Second Sex*. New York: Knopf, 1953 (English translation).

[5] Friedan famously referred to the suburban home as a "comfortable concentration camp" (Chapter 12) and argued that "housewifery expands to fill the time available." - Friedan, Betty. *The Feminine Mystique*. New York: W.W. Norton & Company, 1963.

[6] Butler, Judith. *Gender Trouble: Feminism and the Subversion of Identity*. New York: Routledge, 1990. This is the seminal academic work introducing "performativity" theory, arguing that gender is a performance rather than a biological reality, the logical endpoint of rejecting the Creation order.

The Failure of Complementarianism

In response to this cultural tidal wave, the conservative church developed the term "Complementarianism" in the late 20th century[7]. While well-intentioned, this position often concedes too much ground. It frequently accepts the feminist premise that women may lead in every sphere of society (business, government, education) except for the office of pastor and the role of husband[8]. This creates a theological cognitive dissonance. If a woman can rule over men as a CEO, a judge, or a President, on what basis does the church forbid her from teaching a Sunday School class? The Bible does not present a "soft" hierarchy restricted only to the pulpit. Isaiah 3:12 laments, "Youths oppress My people, and women rule over them." This was not a limited restriction on temple duties. It was a judgment on the nation itself. When men abdicate and women rule, it is a sign of God's judgment, not His blessing. Complementarianism often tries to manage the symptoms of feminism without addressing the root error: the rejection of Father-rule (Patriarchy).

Restoring the Ancient Paths

The church must stop apologizing for God's design. We do not need a "soft" version of hierarchy that tries to appease the culture. We need a robust, biblical theology that embraces the goodness of male headship and female submission. This is not about power for the sake of power. It is about reflecting the order of Christ and the Church. When we compromise on this issue, we discredit the Word of God (Titus 2:5). The path forward is not forward into new progressive compromises, but backward to the ancient paths of the Apostles and Prophets. We must affirm that the man is the head of

---

7 *The Danvers Statement*. Council on Biblical Manhood and Womanhood (CBMW), 1987. This document defines the ideas and defined the movement in response to evangelical feminism.

8 Piper, John, and Wayne Grudem, eds. *Recovering Biblical Manhood and Womanhood*. Wheaton: Crossway, 1991. This is the definitive systematic theology of the Complementarian movement.

the woman, and this order applies to the church, the home, and the ordering of society.

Reflection Questions

1. How does the description of female rule in Isaiah 3:12 as a judgment challenge the modern view that female leadership is a sign of progress?
2. In what ways does the instruction in Titus 2:5 for women to be "managers of their households" conflict with the modern push for career prioritization?
3. How has the church's attempt to accommodate culture through "soft" Complementarianism actually weakened its ability to defend biblical roles of the sexes?

> ***On Rights vs. The Curse:*** *Feminism clamors for rights, but Scripture reveals this impulse as teshuqah, the curse of desire to control the man (Genesis 3:16). This movement is not progress; it is the codification of the curse.*
>
> ***On Duty vs. Disorder:*** *The verdict of Scripture is clear: when women rule, the people are oppressed (Isaiah 3:12). Order is restored only when the woman embraces her duty as manager of the household (Titus 2:5), rejecting the false promise of power for the true virtue of obedience.*

the woman, and the order applies to the church, the home and the ordering in society.

[illegible]

1. How does [illegible] description of [illegible] as [illegible] themselves [illegible] progress?

2. In what ways does the instruction in [illegible] be [illegible] of their households conflict with the modern push [illegible] of civilization?

3. How has the church's attempt to accommodate culture through [illegible] complementarianism actually weakened its ability to uphold biblical roles of the sexes?

[illegible] Scripture [illegible] this impulse [illegible] the [illegible] of desire or control [illegible] (Genesis 3:16). [illegible] is not progress; it is the [illegible] of the curse.

[illegible] Scripture [illegible] oppressed (Isaiah 3:12). Order is restored only when [illegible] the household (Titus 2:5) [illegible] pattern for the [illegible]

7.2 - Philosophers' Partial Truths

Plato, Aristotle, and the Limits of Reason Human reason, as seen in the ancient philosophers, captures fragments of truth about order yet remains flawed and incomplete without God's revealed Word. Without Scripture, the mind of man inevitably drifts into one of two errors regarding the sexes. It either erases the distinctions God created or it degrades the value of the woman God fashioned.

🕮 THE WITNESSES

I. **1 Corinthians 3**
19: "For the wisdom of this world is foolishness in God's sight. As it is written: 'He catches the wise in their craftiness.'"

II. **Jeremiah 8**
9: "The wise will be put to shame; they will be dismayed and trapped. Since they have rejected the word of the Lord, what wisdom do they really have?"

III. **Romans 1**
22: "Although they claimed to be wise, they became fools"

The Limits of Unaided Reason

Many modern critics dismiss the biblical hierarchy of the home as merely a reflection of ancient patriarchal culture. They argue that the Apostles simply borrowed their ideas from the surrounding Greco-Roman world. However, when we examine the writings of the greatest secular minds of antiquity, we find that their views on men and women were radically different from the biblical model.

The ancient philosophers observed nature and society through the lens of fallen human reason. While they occasionally glimpsed the reality of order, they lacked the corrective lens of special revelation.

Scripture subordinates all human wisdom to divine revelation. Paul states plainly in 1 Corinthians 3:19, "For the wisdom of this world is foolishness in God's sight." Human logic, untethered from the fear of the Lord, cannot arrive at the divine balance of functional subordination and ontological equality. As Jeremiah 8:9 asks, "Since they have rejected the word of the LORD, what kind of wisdom do they have?" We must analyze the errors of Plato and Aristotle to see how the Bible stands apart as the only perfect standard.

Plato and the Error of Erasure

The first error is the erasure of distinction in the name of utility. In his work *The Republic*, Plato constructs an ideal society where the nuclear family is abolished among the ruling class. He argues that women should receive the same education as men and perform the same functions, including warfare and governance. Plato acknowledges that women are generally physically weaker, but he contends that their nature is not different in kind from men regarding the capacity for leadership. His solution to the social arrangement of the sexes was to minimize their differences. He sought to strip women of their domestic role so they could serve the state in the same capacity as men[9]. This is the ancient forebear of modern egalitarianism.

Scripture rejects this erasure. Order is not based on competence or capacity. It is based on the created order of God. In 1 Timothy 2:13, Paul does not argue from physical strength or intellectual capacity. He argues from the sequence of creation: "For Adam was

---

[9] Plato argues through Socrates that "the natural capacities are distributed alike among both creatures (men and women), and women naturally share in all offices and men in all." He advocates for women to share in the duties of the Guardian class, including war, arguing that the only difference is that women are weaker in all things, but not different in nature regarding the soul's capacity for virtue or governance. Plato. *Republic*. Translated by G.M.A. Grube. Indianapolis: Hackett Publishing, 1992.

formed first, then Eve." The distinction between man and woman is not a defect to be fixed by education. It is a feature of God's design. By assigning the woman the role of "a suitable helper" (Genesis 2:18), God established a functional difference that no amount of philosophical reasoning can undo. Plato's error was assuming that equality of worth requires sameness of role. The Bible teaches that roles are distinct because the design is distinct.

Aristotle and the Error of Degradation

The second error is the justification of hierarchy through degradation. Aristotle, in his work *Politics*, correctly observed that the household is the fundamental unit of society and that the male is the head of the female. However, his foundation for this rule was flawed. Aristotle argued that the male is by nature superior and the female inferior[10]. He viewed the female as a "deformed male," lacking the full capacity for rationality and authority[11]. For Aristotle, the man rules the woman because she is ontologically lesser than he is. This is the error of chauvinism and tyranny.

Scripture upholds the hierarchy but utterly rejects the degradation. The Bible confirms that "the head of the woman is man" (1 Corinthians 11:3), but it never bases this headship on the idea that women are less human or less intelligent. On the contrary, Genesis 1:27 declares, "So God created man in His own image, in the image of God He created him; male and female He created them." The woman is a full image-bearer of God, equal in essence and worth to the man. The hierarchy of the Bible is not based on the woman's inferiority. It is based on the Creator's assignment.

---

[10] Aristotle distinguishes between different types of rule. He states, "The male is by nature superior, and the female inferior; and the one rules, and the other is ruled." He argues that while the woman has a deliberative faculty, it is "without authority" (*akyron*). Aristotle. *Politics*. Book I, Chapter 12 (1259a–1260a).

[11] Here Aristotle famously describes the female as a "deformed male" (*arren peperōmenon*) or a male that has not developed perfectly due to a lack of heat during conception. Aristotle. *Generation of Animals*. Book II, 737a.

The Biblical Balance

We see then that the Bible walks a path that human reason cannot find on its own. Plato tried to elevate women by making them men. Aristotle tried to keep men in charge by devaluing women. The Bible alone presents the high paradox of the Kingdom. The woman is equal to the man in essence, dignity, and value, yet she is subordinate to him in role and function.

This balance is secured by the Trinitarian archetype found in 1 Corinthians 11:3: "the head of every man is Christ, and the head of the woman is man, and the head of Christ is God." Just as Christ is not inferior to the Father in essence but submits to Him in authority, the wife is not inferior to the husband in being but submits to his headship. We do not need the errors of the philosophers[12]. We have the Word of God which establishes order without tyranny and distinction without degradation.

Reflection Questions

1. How does Plato's argument for women performing the same roles as men mirror modern egalitarian arguments regarding the interchangeability of the sexes?
2. Why is it dangerous to defend male headship using Aristotle's logic of female inferiority rather than the biblical logic of creation order?
3. How does 1 Corinthians 11:3 provide the solution that both Plato and Aristotle missed regarding equality of essence and distinction of authority?

---

[12] Prudence Allen. *The Concept of Woman: The Aristotelian Revolution, 750 BC–AD 1250*. Grand Rapids: Eerdmans, 1997. This work provides a detailed comparison of Plato's "unitarian" view (erasing distinction) versus Aristotle's "polarity" view (creating inferiority), contrasting both with the Christian "complementarity" (integral) view.

On Philosophy: *"The world oscillates between making women into men (Plato) and making women into slaves (Aristotle). Only the Bible treats them as women. It treats them as queens in their own domain, under the cover of their head."*

On Reason: *"Human reason is a useful servant but a terrible master. When we use reason to judge Scripture, we end up with the errors of the age. When we use Scripture to judge reason, we find the mind of Christ."*

7.3 - Church Leaders' Reflections on Order

Church leaders throughout history have affirmed the biblical order of male headship and female submission as divine design. While their writings serve only to illuminate Scripture, their unified testimony confirms that the egalitarian rejection of hierarchy is a modern deviation from the historic Christian faith.

🕮 THE WITNESSES

I. **1 Corinthians 11**
 3: "But I want you to understand that the head of every man is Christ, and the head of the woman is man, and the head of Christ is God."

II. **Ephesians 5**
 23: "For the husband is the head of the wife as Christ is the head of the church, His body, of which He is the Savior."

III. **1 Timothy 2**
 12: "I do not permit a woman to teach or to exercise authority over a man; she is to remain quiet."

The Historic Witness to Divine Order

Modern critics often claim that the concept of male headship is a result of patriarchal oppression or cultural backwardness. They argue that the church must "evolve" beyond the views of the past to embrace a new egalitarian standard. However, when we look at the giants of the faith, we find a unified voice. From the early church fathers to the Reformers and the great preachers of the 19th century, the consensus is clear. They did not view hierarchy as oppression. They viewed it as the structure of creation and the command of God.

While these men are not our ultimate authority, as only Scripture holds that place, their agreement confirms that the egalitarian reading is a modern novelty. It was unknown to the vast majority of church history. By examining their reflections on the witnesses provided, we see that they understood *kephale* (head) and *hupotasso* (submit) exactly as the Apostles intended.

John Chrysostom and the Order of Authority

> *"The wife is a second authority; let not her then demand equality, for she is under the head; nor let him despise her as being in subjection, for she is the body; and if the head despise the body, it will perish with it." — Homily 20 on Ephesians*[13]

John Chrysostom (c. 347-407 AD), preaching in the late fourth century, provided one of the clearest patristic expositions of divine hierarchy as rooted in creation rather than culture.

In his Homily 20 on Ephesians, commenting on Ephesians 5:23 ("For the husband is the head of the wife as Christ is the head of the church, His body, of which He is the Savior"), Chrysostom declared that headship reflects the unchanging order established before the fall: the husband leads in love, the wife submits in reverence, mirroring Christ and the church.

Most notably, in Homily 9 on 1 Timothy, addressing 1 Timothy 2:12 ("I do not permit a woman to teach or to exercise authority over a man; she is to remain quiet."), Chrysostom tied the prohibition directly to Genesis:

---

[13] Chrysostom, John. *Homily 20 on Ephesians*. Translated by Gross Alexander. From *Nicene and Post-Nicene Fathers*, First Series, Vol. 13. Edited by Philip Schaff. Buffalo, NY: Christian Literature Publishing Co., 1889.

> *"The woman taught once, and ruined all. On this account therefore he says, let her not teach. But what is it to other women, that she suffered this? It certainly concerns them; for the sex is weak and fickle, and he is speaking of the sex collectively."*[14]

He immediately grounded this in pre-fall creation order:

> *"For God made her subject from the beginning... 'Thy desire shall be to thy husband, and he shall rule over thee' (Genesis 3:16)."*

Yet he balanced it with equality in essence: both bear God's image and share equal honor in Christ. Chrysostom's exegesis thus continued the apostolic pattern. Hierarchy in role is creation-based, binding on the church in every age, not a temporary concession to Roman or Jewish custom.

Augustine and the Trinitarian Reflection

> *"Domestic peace is the well-ordered concord between those of the family who rule and those who obey. For they who care for the rest rule... and they who are cared for obey." — The City of God, Book 19, Chapter 14*[15]

Augustine of Hippo (354–430), perhaps the most influential theologian of the West, rooted the order of the sexes in the nature of God's peace. He defined peace as the "tranquility of order." For Augustine, order is not tyranny; it is the arrangement of things equal and unequal, assigning to each its proper place.

He saw the relationship between the man and the woman as a reflection of this divine order. Just as the soul rules the body, the husband rules the wife; not for his own advantage, but for her good. He argued that sin disrupted this peaceful order, introducing conflict, but that the Christian home is called to restore it. The

---

[14] Chrysostom, John. *Homily 9 on 1 Timothy*. In *Nicene and Post-Nicene Fathers*, First Series, Vol. 13. Edited by Philip Schaff. Buffalo, NY: Christian Literature Publishing Co., 1889.

[15] Augustine. *The City of God*. Book 19, Chapter 14. Translated by Marcus Dods. From *Nicene and Post-Nicene Fathers*, First Series, Vol. 2. Edited by Philip Schaff. Buffalo, NY: Christian Literature Publishing Co., 1887.

husband's authority is an office of service and love, yet it is a true authority that must be obeyed for the sake of domestic peace.

John Calvin and the Creation Ordinance

> *"God did not create two chiefs of equal power, but added to the man an inferior aid... For the woman is constituted, to be in subjection to the man." — Commentary on 1 Timothy 2:12-13*[16]

The great Reformer John Calvin (1509–1564) was unwavering in his exposition of 1 Timothy 2. He rejected the idea that Paul's commands were merely local customs for Ephesus. Calvin anchored his argument in 1 Timothy 2:13, which states, "For Adam was formed first, and then Eve."

For Calvin, the order of creation established an eternal law. He taught that for a woman to usurp the place of teaching or authority over a man was a violation of the order of nature established by God. He upheld the apostolic command that women are not permitted to teach men. This was not misogyny to Calvin. It was obedience to the divine arrangement. He argued that since God assigned the man the role of headship before the Fall, no amount of redemption removes that natural order in this life.

---

[16] Calvin, John. *Commentaries on the Epistles to Timothy, Titus, and Philemon.* On 1 Timothy 2:12. Translated by William Pringle. Grand Rapids: Eerdmans, 1948. The term "inferior" in this translation is used in the sense of "subordinate in rank" (*inferior* in Latin), consistent with the 16th-century theological context of order, not necessarily essence.

Charles Spurgeon and the Holiness of the Home

> *"The husband is the head of the wife... He is the king, she is the queen; but he is the king. When there are two kings, there is sure to be war; and when there are two heads to the household, the house will soon be a ruin." — Sermon: The Marriage of the Lamb*[17]

Charles Spurgeon (1834–1892), the "Prince of Preachers," spoke often of the beauty of the Christian home. He warned against movements in his day that sought to erase distinctions between the sexes. He preached that a happy home is built on the husband's loving leadership and the wife's gracious support.

He saw the husband's headship as a heavy responsibility to care for the wife, referencing Ephesians 5:23. He saw the wife's submission as a place of honor and influence, not of servitude. To Spurgeon, the husband is the "house-band"; the band that holds the house together. When the husband fails to lead or the wife refuses to submit, the band snaps, and the home disintegrates.

The Consensus of the Faithful

We are not the first generation to read the Bible. When we embrace male headship and female submission, we stand in a long line of faithful witnesses. Chrysostom, Augustine, Calvin, and Spurgeon were in agreement. They recognized that 1 Corinthians 11:3 establishes a chain that cannot be broken without consequence. We do not follow them as masters, but we walk with them as brothers who heard the same voice of the Shepherd. The "progress" of modern egalitarianism is actually a regression into disorder, rejecting the wisdom of the ages for the whims of the present culture.

---

[17] Spurgeon, C.H. "The Marriage of the Lamb." Sermon No. 2096. Delivered July 21, 1889, at the Metropolitan Tabernacle. *Metropolitan Tabernacle Pulpit*, Vol. 35. London: Passmore & Alabaster, 1889.

Reflection Questions

1. How does Augustine's definition of peace as "well-ordered concord" change the way we view submission in the home?
2. Why is it significant that Calvin rooted his argument in the order of creation (Adam formed first) rather than just the culture of his day?
3. How does knowing that the vast majority of church history supports male headship give us confidence to stand against modern cultural pressure?

> ***On Tradition:*** *"Tradition is the democracy of the dead. It means giving a vote to the most obscure of all classes, our ancestors. We refuse to let the arrogance of the present silence the wisdom of the past."*
>
> ***On Consensus:*** *"When the church fathers, the reformers, and the puritans all agree on a plain reading of Scripture, we should tremble before we invent a new interpretation to please the modern world."*

7.4 - Societal Collapses from Inversion

Rome, Israel, and the Modern West The inversion of divine hierarchy, wherein women assume authority over men and traditional roles are reversed, is not a mark of progress but a specific form of divine judgment that precedes societal collapse. This pattern is evidenced in the biblical record of ancient Israel, the historical decline of the Roman Empire, and the current trajectory of the modern West.

🕮 THE WITNESSES

I. **Isaiah 3**
12: "Youths oppress My people, and women rule over them. O My people, your guides mislead you; they turn you from your paths."

II. **Genesis 3**
16: "To the woman He said: 'I will sharply increase your pain in childbirth; in pain you will bring forth children. Your desire will be for your husband, and he will rule over you.'"

III. **Malachi 4**
6: "And he will turn the hearts of the fathers to their children, and the hearts of the children to their fathers. Otherwise, I will come and strike the land with a curse."

The Anatomy of Collapse

Patterns of societal decline frequently involve the erosion of family structures and role distinctions. While secular historians often note these trends as mere cultural shifts, Scripture identifies them as mechanisms of divine judgment. When the created order of male headship is subverted, society does not merely change. It loses its structural integrity. The Bible does not describe a society where women rule as enlightened or progressive. It describes it as a society under judgment where the natural protectors have abdicated and confusion reigns.

God's judgment often takes the form of giving a people over to their own desires. When men refuse to rule under submission to the will of God, God removes them. The result is a vacuum of authority that is filled by those not designed for the burden of primary governance. This inversion creates a culture where emotion supersedes reason and safety is sacrificed for autonomy.

The Biblical Pattern of Judgment

The primary witness, Isaiah 3:12, provides a chilling diagnosis of a collapsing society. God declares, "Youths oppress My people, and women rule over them. O My people, your guides mislead you; they turn you from your paths."

Context is vital here. In the preceding verses of Isaiah 3, God removes the "mighty man and the warrior" (Isaiah 3:2). The removal of capable, godly male leadership creates a void. Into this void step "youths" and "women." The pairing is significant. The oppression by youths represents immaturity, emotion, and rebellion against wisdom. This parallels the rule of women, representing the inversion of the creation order. In the biblical worldview, a society where women exercise authority over men is a society that has lost its men. It serves as a sign that the men have failed to be what they were created to be. This inversion is not a blessing of equality. It is a curse of disorder that leads a people astray.

The Perpetual Conflict

The root of this tension traces back to the Garden. The second witness explains the dynamic. In Genesis 3:16, God tells the woman, "Your desire will be for your husband, and he will rule over you."

As discussed in Chapter 4.2, the Hebrew word for "desire" (*teshuqah*) implies a desire to control or master. Remember, it's the same word used in Genesis 4:7 describing sin's desire to master Cain. The curse introduces a conflict where the woman seeks to usurp the man's position, and the man must rule (*mashal*) over her, often leading to conflict or tyranny. History is the record of this struggle. When a culture encourages the woman's *teshuqah* to dominate, it invites the chaos of the Fall into its very foundations. The modern celebration of female empowerment over men is simply the public institutionalization of the curse of Eve.

Inversion in Ancient Israel

We see this collapse vividly in the era of the Judges. The text tells us repeatedly that "In those days there was no king in Israel; everyone did what was right in his own eyes" (Judges 21:25).

This era culminates in the horrific inversion of Judges 19. A Levite man allows his concubine to be abused to save himself. This is the ultimate inversion of headship. The man, who is designed to protect, sacrifices the woman to protect himself. This atrocity occurred because male leadership had collapsed into passivity and selfishness. It led to civil war and the near annihilation of the tribe of Benjamin. When men fail to rule their households and the land according to God's law, the result is not freedom. It is anarchy and destruction.

The Decline of Rome

Historical accounts of Rome's fall highlight a similar pattern. In the early Republic, the *paterfamilias* (father of the family) held absolute authority, and the family unit was strong. As the empire declined, this structure eroded[18]. Laws were changed to grant women independent property rights and the ability to divorce easily. The "new woman" of the late Empire sought independence from the authority of fathers and husbands.

As the family collapsed from within due to role inversion and moral[19] decay, the state lost the civic virtue necessary to survive. Rome did not fall simply because of barbarian invasions. It fell because the internal order of the home had already been sacked by the abandonment of natural law[20]. A society that cannot govern its own households cannot govern an empire. The feminization of the culture led to a loss of martial strength and disciplined order.

The Modern West and the Curse

Today, we see the ultimate fruit of this inversion in the West. We face an epidemic of fatherlessness[21]. The collapse of the nuclear family is no longer a theoretical risk but a statistical reality. According to the National Vital Statistics Reports released in 2025, covering final data for 2023, the percentage of all births to unmarried women in the United States stands at 40.0%[22].

This fragmentation is even more severe in specific demographics, with nonmarital birth rates reaching as high as 69.3% in some groups. In certain states, such as Louisiana and Mississippi, more than one in two children are born to unmarried mothers. This

---

[18] Zimmerman, Carle C. *Family and Civilization*. New York: Harper & Brothers, 1947. Zimmerman outlines the transition from the "trustee family" (strong clan authority) to the "domestic family" (strong nuclear family) to the "atomistic family" (individualism). He correlates the rise of the atomistic family, marked by easy divorce, feminism, and loss of *patria potestas*, with the collapse of Greek and Roman civilizations.

[19] Juvenal. *Satire VI*. (Circa 1st/2nd Century AD). A satirical but historically relevant critique of the changing morals and independence of Roman women in the Empire period, reflecting the shift away from traditional domestic roles.

[20] Unwin, J.D. *Sex and Culture*. London: Oxford University Press, 1934. Unwin's anthropological study of 86 civilizations concludes that cultures lose their "expansive energy" within three generations of abandoning absolute monogamy and pre-nuptial chastity.

[21] Popenoe, David. *Life Without Father: Compelling New Evidence That Fatherhood and Marriage Are Indispensable for the Good of Children and Society*. New York: Free Press, 1996. Defines the social cost of the decline of fatherhood.

[22] Osterman MJK, Hamilton BE, Martin JA, Driscoll AK, Valenzuela CP. *Births: Final Data for 2023*. National Vital Statistics Reports; vol 74 no 1. Hyattsville, MD: National Center for Health Statistics. 2025.

is not merely a different family structure. It is a broken one. The removal of the father from the home correlates with societal ills including increased crime, behavioral disorders, and poverty. It reflects the warning of the third witness, Malachi 4:6: "Otherwise, I will come and strike the land with a curse." The restoration of society depends on the restoration of the father. When headship is abandoned and the hearts of fathers are turned away from their duty, the land is struck. We are living in the struck land.

The Path to Restoration

Inversion is no accident. It is the fruit of judgment. We must reject the cultural celebration of role reversal and return to the biblical standard. This requires repentance. Fathers must turn their hearts to their children. Husbands must lead with love and strength. Wives must submit with reverence. Churches must teach uncompromised order. We cannot build a stable society on the foundation of rebellion. Obedience to God's hierarchy is the only path to averting the curse and rebuilding the ruins.

Reflection Questions

1. How does the account of the Levite's concubine in Judges 19 illustrate the extreme consequences of a society where men fail to lead and protect?
2. In light of Genesis 3:16 and Malachi 4:6, why is the modern epidemic of fatherlessness a theological crisis rather than just a social one?
3. How does the historical erosion of the *paterfamilias* in Rome serve as a warning to the modern church regarding the ideology of role reversal?

> ***On Civilization:*** *"Civilization is built on the backs of men who take responsibility. When men lay down that burden to pursue pleasure, and women pick up that burden to pursue power, the civilization dies."*
>
> ***On Judgment:*** *"We think female rule is progress. God calls it judgment. We cannot bless what God has defined as a sign of a stumbling nation."*

7.5 - The Early Church on Hierarchy

Apostolic Fathers to Nicaea The early church, spanning from the Apostolic Fathers to the Council of Nicaea, universally upheld the biblical hierarchy of male headship and female submission in both the home and the assembly. This historical consensus confirms that the "cultural accommodation" view is a modern invention foreign to the apostolic mind.

🕮 THE WITNESSES

I. **1 Corinthians 11**
 10: "For this reason a woman ought to have a sign of authority on her head, because of the angels."

II. **Ephesians 5**
 23: "For the husband is the head of the wife as Christ is the head of the church, His body, of which He is the Savior."

III. **1 Timothy 3**
 2: "An overseer, then, must be above reproach, the husband of but one wife, temperate, self-controlled, respectable, hospitable, able to teach,"

The Continuity of Apostolic Doctrine

Modern egalitarian theology often suggests that Paul's restrictions on women were temporary cultural concessions that the "spirit of the text" intended to eventually overcome. If this were true, we would expect to see the church moving toward egalitarianism immediately after the Apostles died. We find the exact opposite.

The writings of the early church provide historical continuity with apostolic doctrine. They offer insights into how hierarchy was practiced amid persecution and the rise of heresy. While Scripture alone establishes order, the uniform testimony of the early church subordinates all modern novelties to the ancient path.

The Apostolic Fathers: Clement and Ignatius

> *"Let wives be subject to their husbands in the fear of God; and let the husbands love their wives as Christ also loved the Church." — Epistle to the Philadelphians (Ignatius)*[23]

The leaders who immediately succeeded the Apostles maintained this order without apology. Clement of Rome (c. 96 AD), writing to the Corinthians regarding order and rebellion, urged harmony through submission. He did not view the hierarchy of the home or the church as a result of the Fall but as a reflection of the Creator's design.

Ignatius of Antioch (c. 110 AD), a disciple of the Apostle John, instructed wives to submit in purity and husbands to love as Christ. He viewed the bishop's authority as a reflection of God the Father. For Ignatius, the structure of the church was masculine and paternal, mirroring the divine Fatherhood. He explicitly tied male leadership in the church to the nature of God, not to the culture of Rome.

---

[23] Ignatius. *Epistle to the Philadelphians*. Chapter 4. (Long Recension). In *The Ante-Nicene Fathers*, Vol. 1. Edited by Alexander Roberts and James Donaldson. Buffalo, NY: Christian Literature Publishing Co., 1885.

Pre-Nicene Fathers: Tertullian and Origen

> *"It is not permitted to a woman to speak in church... neither does she teach, nor baptize, nor offer, nor claim to herself a lot in any manly function, not to mention the priestly office."*
> *— On the Veiling of Virgins (Tertullian)*[24]

As the church expanded, the defense of order continued against paganism and gnosticism. Tertullian (c. 200 AD) wrote extensively on the creation order. In his work *On the Veiling of Virgins*, he argued from 1 Corinthians 11 that the covering was a sign of submission and authority. He contended that because angels (1 Corinthians 11:10) witness the order, the woman must maintain her sign of subjection. He strictly prohibited women from public speaking, teaching, or baptizing in the church, citing the apostolic rule as an unchangeable law.

Origen (c. 230 AD) also upheld the silence of women in the assembly based on 1 Timothy 2. While he acknowledged that women could have the gift of prophecy, he distinguished prophecy from the office of teaching. Teaching involves exercising authority over men, which is forbidden. He noted that even the prophetesses in Scripture did not speak in the assembly of men, maintaining the distinction between private edification and public authority.

Continuity into the Late Fourth Century

The consensus did not waver even as the church entered the late fourth century. John Chrysostom (c. 347-407 AD), preaching shortly after the Council of Nicaea's influence had settled, defended the same creation-based hierarchy.

As examined in greater depth in Chapter 7.3, Chrysostom explicitly rooted both male headship (1 Corinthians 11:3; Ephesians 5:23) and the prohibition on women exercising authoritative teaching over men (1 Timothy 2:12) in the pre-fall order of Genesis,

---

[24] Tertullian. *On the Veiling of Virgins* (*De Virginibus Velandis*). Chapter 9. In *The Ante-Nicene Fathers*, Vol. 4.

specifically Eve's derivation from Adam and the consequent divine arrangement, rather than in passing Greco-Roman customs. He viewed these instructions as timeless ordinances, binding on the church universally.

This late-fourth-century witness confirms that the apostolic tradition remained intact: the early church's uniform reading of the witness passages endured without dilution.

The Nicene Era and Apostolic Continuity

The Council of Nicaea (325 AD) focused primarily on the deity of Christ, yet the structure of the council itself testified to the male-only priesthood. The attendees were bishops, men appointed to oversee the church. This was not an accident of history. It was obedience to Scripture.

1 Timothy 3:2 states, "An overseer, then, must be above reproach, the husband of but one wife, temperate, self-controlled, respectable, hospitable, able to teach," The early church understood this requirement literally and functionally. They rejected female elders or teachers because they contradicted the qualifications found in Scripture. Just as Christ submits to the Father without loss of essence, the woman submits to the man. The church fathers understood that tampering with the order of the sexes eventually leads to tampering with the order of the Trinity.

The Unbroken Chain of Antiquity

The witness of the early church is unanimous. From the first century through the fourth, the church understood male headship and female submission as the revealed will of God. They did not view 1 Timothy 2:12 or Ephesians 5:23 as cultural artifacts of the first century. They viewed them as creation ordinances binding on all generations. We stand on firm historical ground when we uphold this order today.

Reflection Questions

1. How does the testimony of Clement and Ignatius refute the idea that male headship was a later corruption of the church?
2. Why is Tertullian's connection between 1 Corinthians 11 (angels) and the behavior of women in the church significant for our worship today?
3. Building on the fuller treatment in Chapter 7.3, how did John Chrysostom extend the early church's consistent practice of grounding the prohibition on women teaching authoritative doctrine to men in the pre-fall Genesis account rather than in transient cultural conditions?

> ***On History:*** *"We are not the first to read the Bible. When we ignore 2,000 years of church history to invent a new 'egalitarian' interpretation, we are not being enlightened. We are being arrogant."*
>
> ***On Order:*** *"The early church faced persecution, heresy, and death. They did not survive by compromising God's order. They survived by obeying it."*

7.6 - Early Church vs. Proto-Egalitarianism

Montanism, Gnosticism, and Suppression Early heresies such as Montanism and Gnosticism elevated women into authoritative roles under claims of new revelation or spiritual equality, inverting biblical order. The orthodox church rightly suppressed these movements not out of cultural bias, but to align with Scripture's prohibition on women teaching doctrine over men, distinguishing lawful prophecy from unlawful authority.

🕮 THE WITNESSES

I. **1 Timothy 2**
12: "I do not permit a woman to teach or to exercise authority over a man; she is to remain quiet."

II. **1 Corinthians 11**
5: "And every woman who prays or prophesies with her head uncovered dishonors her head, for it is just as if her head were shaved."

III. **2 Timothy 3**
6-7: "They are the kind who worm their way into households and captivate vulnerable women who are weighed down with sins and led astray by various passions, who are always learning but never able to come to a knowledge of the truth."

The Heretical Roots of Egalitarianism

Modern egalitarian historians often argue that the early church was originally egalitarian but later "patriarchalized" by men seeking power. They point to groups in the second and third centuries where women held leadership roles as evidence of a "lost Christianity." However, a closer examination reveals that these groups were not the orthodox church of the Apostles. They were the heretics the Apostles warned against.

The push for female authority in the early church almost always accompanied a departure from the authority of Scripture or the goodness of creation. Two primary movements, Montanism and Gnosticism, exemplify this rebellion. The church's rejection of their practices was a defense of the apostolic deposit found in the primary witness, 1 Timothy 2:12.

Montanism: Enthusiastic Prophecy Leading to Inversion

Montanism, also known as the "New Prophecy," emerged in the late second century. Led by Montanus and two prophetesses, Prisca and Maximilla, this movement claimed that the Holy Spirit was giving new revelations that superseded the authority of the local bishops and the apostolic writings. Because they elevated subjective experience above the objective Word, they dismantled the biblical distinctions of order.

Women in Montanism were permitted to teach and exercise authority based on their "prophetic" status. The orthodox church fathers rejected this, not because they despised prophecy, but because they understood the biblical distinction[25]. While women could prophesy, as seen in 1 Corinthians 11:5, they were forbidden from the authoritative office of teaching or ruling[26]. Montanism blurred this line, allowing emotionalism to override the command for women to "remain quiet" in the assembly (1 Timothy 2:12).

---

[25] Eusebius. *Ecclesiastical History*. Book 5, Chapters 16-19. Eusebius records the church's rejection of Montanus and his prophetesses, viewing their ecstatic, authoritative utterances as contrary to the apostolic tradition.

[26] Epiphanius of Salamis. *Panarion* (Medicine Chest). Section 49. Epiphanius critiques the Montanists (Quintillians) for ordaining women as bishops and presbyters, citing Eve's deception as the reason for the prohibition.

Gnosticism: Spiritual Equality Denying Creation Order

Gnosticism was a diverse set of heresies that generally taught that the physical world was evil and the spirit was good. Consequently, they despised the physical distinctions between male and female, viewing them as traps of the material world. Gnostic texts often elevated female figures like Mary Magdalene as the recipients of secret knowledge (*gnosis*), claiming she had insight superior to the male apostles.

However, this "equality" was based on a rejection of creation. The Gnostic "Gospel of Thomas" (saying 114) famously claims that for a woman to enter the Kingdom, she must make herself "male."[27] This is a denial of Genesis 1:27. The orthodox church stood firm on the goodness of the physical creation and the permanent validity of the male-female distinction. By rejecting Gnosticism, the church affirmed that God's order is good and that the distinct roles of men and women are not a curse to be escaped but a design to be lived.

The Target of Deception

The third witness, 2 Timothy 3:6-7, provides a sobering insight into how heresy spreads. It warns of those who "worm their way into households and captivate vulnerable women... always learning but never able to come to a knowledge of the truth."

Historically, false teachers have often targeted women to gain a foothold in the church[28]. By exploiting the emotional nature or the desire for spiritual significance, heresies like Montanism empowered women to usurp authority, leading entire households astray. The orthodox defense of male headship was a protective

[27] *The Gospel of Thomas*. Saying 114. (Nag Hammadi Library). "Simon Peter said to them, 'Make Mary leave us, for females don't deserve life.' Jesus said, 'Look, I will guide her to make her male, so that she too may become a living spirit resembling you males. For every female who makes herself male will enter the kingdom of heaven.'" (Used to illustrate the Gnostic rejection of female ontology).

[28] Irenaeus. *Against Heresies*. Book 1, Chapter 13. Irenaeus describes the Gnostic teacher Marcus, who deceived many women, leading them into both spiritual error and sexual immorality.

measure against this deception, ensuring that the church remained grounded in the "knowledge of the truth" rather than being swept away by "various passions."[29]

Conclusion to Part IV

We have traversed the landscape of history, from the feminist revolutions of the modern era back to the heresies of the second century. The testimony is consistent.

- **Feminism (7.1)** rebelled against the curse.
- **Philosophy (7.2)** lacked the light of revelation.
- **Church Leaders (7.3)** affirmed the apostolic order.
- **Societal Collapse (7.4)** demonstrated the consequences of inversion.
- **The Early Church (7.5)** upheld the hierarchy of creation.
- **Heresy (7.6)** attempted to dismantle it.

History confirms what Scripture commands. The order of male headship and female submission is the heartbeat of a healthy church and society. Those who reject it do not march toward progress, but drift toward ancient errors.

As we move into **Part V**, we will confront the modern distortions directly. We will see how these ancient errors have been repackaged in the 21st century, infiltrating the church under the guise of "justice" and "equality," and we will arm ourselves with the biblical counter-arguments necessary to stand firm.

[29] Tertullian. *On the Veiling of Virgins*. Chapter 9. Tertullian explicitly forbids women from speaking in church, teaching, baptizing, or assuming any function that belongs to men, specifically the priestly office, in response to heretical practices.

Reflection Questions

1. How does the distinction between "prophecy" and "teaching authority" help explain why the church rejected Montanist practices?
2. In what ways does modern egalitarianism resemble Gnosticism in its view of the physical body and the distinctions of the sexes?
3. Why is 2 Timothy 3:6-7 a critical warning for the church today regarding how false teaching often enters a community?

> ***On Heresy:*** *"Heresy is not just bad theology; it is mutiny against God's order. Every time the church has embraced female leadership, it has eventually abandoned the authority of Scripture."*
>
> ***On Protection:*** *"Male headship is a wall of fire around the church. When we tear it down in the name of equality, we let the wolves in."*

PART V: MODERN DISTORTIONS AND BIBLICAL COUNTER

Chapter 8: Modern Distortions - Misinterpretations and Consequences

8.1 - Debunking Egalitarian Arguments

Subversion, Extrabiblical Claims, and Textual Twisting

We now enter **Part V: Modern Distortions and Biblical Counter**. Building on the foundational refutation of egalitarian and matriarchal claims in Chapter 2.2 and the apostolic distinctions established in Chapter 6.2, this chapter now confronts the specific textual twists and extrabiblical appeals that dominate modern discourse.

Having established the foundation of order in Creation (Part I), the interruption of the Fall (Part II), the unified witness of Scripture (Part III), and the testimony of history (Part IV), we must now confront the specific arguments used to dismantle this doctrine in our time. The modern church is besieged by interpretations that seek to harmonize the Bible with secular egalitarianism. These arguments do not arise from the text itself but are imposed upon it. We begin by dismantling the primary mechanisms used to subvert God's hierarchy.

Egalitarian claims erode divine hierarchy by subverting texts like Galatians 3:28, importing extrabiblical ideas of equality in role, and twisting terms like *kephale* and *authentein*. These arguments contradict Scripture's consistent witnesses for male positional authority and female submission.

🕮 THE WITNESSES

I. **Galatians 3**
 28: "There is neither Jew nor Greek, slave nor free, male nor female, for you are all one in Christ Jesus.."

II. **1 Timothy 6**
 1: "All who are under the yoke of slavery should regard

their masters as fully worthy of honor, so that God's name and our teaching will not be discredited."

III. **Ephesians 5**

21: "Submit to one another out of reverence for Christ."

Misuse of Salvation Equality to Erase Roles

Many today appeal to equality passages for role interchangeability, finding comfort in interpretations that align with cultural values of autonomy. However, Scripture maintains positional distinctions in role while affirming equality of essence. The egalitarian argument relies on a confusion of categories. It conflates spiritual standing with functional office.

Galatians 3:28 and Soteriology

As addressed in Chapter 2.2, egalitarians frequently cite Galatians 3:28 as the "Magna Carta" of Christian equality, claiming it abolishes all role distinctions. The text states, "There is neither Jew nor Greek, slave nor free, male nor female, for you are all one in Christ Jesus."

However, the context of this passage is strictly soteriological. It concerns who can be saved and become an heir of the promise. Verse 29 concludes, "And if you belong to Christ, then you are Abraham's seed and heirs according to the promise." This passage confirms that access to God is open to all, but it does not dismantle the created order.

The Persistence of Distinctions

If Galatians 3:28 removed all distinctions, we would expect the rest of the New Testament to reflect a role-less society. Instead, we find the Apostles reinforcing distinctions within the body of believers. In 1 Timothy 6:1, Paul commands, "All who are under the yoke of slavery should regard their masters as fully worthy of honor..." Likewise, wives are commanded to submit to their husbands, as seen in Ephesians 5:22. The brotherhood was real, yet the social and functional distinctions remained operative. Therefore, unity in Christ does not negate the hierarchy of the home or the church.

Twisting "Mutual Submission" (Ephesians 5:21)

A common strategy to neutralize male headship is the appeal to "mutual submission" based on Ephesians 5:21, which says, "Submit to one another out of reverence for Christ." It is argued that this general command cancels the specific authority of the husband.

Contextualizing the Participle

Grammatically, verse 21 serves as a bridge. It describes the general attitude of the Spirit-filled community. However, immediately following this, Paul defines how that submission looks in specific relationships. He does not command husbands to submit to wives. Instead, he commands, "Wives, submit to your husbands as to the Lord" (Ephesians 5:22). The specific command clarifies the general principle.

The Direction of Authority

Scripture never commands a husband to submit to his wife, nor a parent to a child, nor Christ to the church. The flow of authority is consistent. In Ephesians 5:23, Paul grounds this not in culture but in theology. He states, "For the husband is the head of the wife as Christ is the head of the church, His body, of which He is the Savior." Just as the church is subject to Christ, the wife is subject to the husband. To argue for mutual submission in terms of authority is to argue that Christ submits to the church, which contradicts the analogy. This is confirmed by Peter, who writes, "Wives, in the same way, submit yourselves to your husbands" (1 Peter 3:1).

Redefining Kephale and Authentein

When the plain text contradicts egalitarian theology, the definitions of words are often challenged. Two key Greek terms, *kephale* (head) and *authentein* (exercise authority), are frequently redefined to remove the connotation of leadership.

Kephale as Authority (1 Corinthians 11:3)

It is often argued that *kephale* means "source" (like the head of a river) rather than "authority over." While *kephale* can imply source, in the context of hierarchy, source implies authority. Paul writes, "But I want you to understand that the head of every man is Christ, and the head of the woman is man, and the head of Christ is God" (1 Corinthians 11:3).

Even if one interprets this as "source," the theology of derivation establishes that the one from whom existence flows holds authority over the derivative. Christ is the head of the church, as stated in Ephesians 5:23, and He certainly exercises authority over it.

Authentein and the Prohibition to Teach (1 Timothy 2:12)

In 1 Timothy 2:12, Paul writes, "I do not permit a woman to teach or to exercise authority over a man." The word for "exercise authority" is *authentein*. Egalitarians often claim this refers to "usurping" or "abusive" authority, implying that positive authority is permitted. However, Paul prohibits the thing itself, not just its abuse.

He grounds this prohibition in the order of creation, not in a local abuse of power. He writes in verses 13 and 14, "For Adam was formed first, and then Eve. And Adam was not the one deceived; it was the woman who was deceived and fell into transgression." The prohibition stands on the pillars of creation priority and the deception of the Fall, rendering it a universal creation ordinance.

The Authority of the Plain Text

Egalitarian arguments rely on subverting specific commands with general principles and redefining clear terms to fit modern sensibilities. However, the witnesses of Scripture remain firm. The order established in creation, confirmed in the law, and modeled by Christ is not erased by our unity in salvation. The plain reading of the text requires us to accept that God has designed different roles for men and women. We must reject these distortions and submit to the plain teaching of the Word, trusting that God's hierarchy is good, necessary, and enduring.

Yet, this truth is often silenced. As we move to the next chapter, we will see how the church's failure to speak these things clearly has led to suppressed voices and significant failures within the body of Christ.

Reflection Questions

1. How does the distinction between "standing in Christ" (Galatians 3:28) and "role in the body" (1 Timothy 2:12) help resolve the tension between equality and hierarchy?
2. Why is the order of creation (Adam formed first) a critical argument against the idea that Paul's commands were merely temporary cultural fixes?
3. If *kephale* implies "source," how does the relationship between God the Father and Christ (1 Corinthians 11:3) demonstrate that "source" still includes authority?

> ***On Salvation vs. Role:*** *"Galatians 3:28 describes our inheritance in heaven. 1 Timothy 2:12 describes our duty on earth. Confusing the two leads to chaos in the church and the home."*
>
> ***On Mutual Submission:*** *"If 'mutual submission' means husbands must obey wives, then Christ must obey the Church. The parallel collapses immediately. We submit to Christ; He does not submit to us."*

8.2 - Suppressed Voices and Church Failures

When Truth Is Silenced Having confronted the arguments that subvert hierarchy in the previous chapter, this section examines the spiritual consequences when the church silences the biblical truth of male headship and female submission established in Chapters 2.1 and 6.2.

Churches that suppress or silence the biblical truth of male headship and female submission invite failure and judgment. By heaping up teachers to suit their own passions rather than enduring sound doctrine, they fulfill the prophetic warnings of Scripture and leave the flock vulnerable to the chaos of inversion.

🕮 THE WITNESSES

I. **2 Timothy 4**
 3-4: "For the time will come when men will not tolerate sound doctrine, but with itching ears they will gather around themselves teachers to suit their own desires. So they will turn their ears away from the truth and turn aside to myths."

II. **Isaiah 30**
 10: "They say to the seers, 'Stop seeing visions!' and to the prophets, 'Do not prophesy to us the truth! Speak to us pleasant words; prophesy illusions.'"

III. **Isaiah 3**
 12: "Youths oppress My people, and women rule over them. O My people, your guides mislead you; they turn you from your paths."

The Culture of Silence

A strange silence has fallen over the modern pulpit regarding the created order of men and women. While the world loudly proclaims the interchangeability of the sexes, the church often retreats into ambiguity. Many pastors avoid the topics of headship and submission to prevent offense, maintain attendance, or appease the culture. However, Scripture warns that the suppression of truth leads not to peace but to deception and ruin.

The Prophecy of Distortion

Paul foretells a specific spiritual condition where the appetite for truth is replaced by an appetite for affirmation. The primary witness, 2 Timothy 4:3, states that "the time will come when men will not tolerate sound doctrine, but with itching ears they will gather around themselves teachers to suit their own desires."

The rejection of the Creator's order regarding men and women is a primary symptom of this intolerance. The doctrine of male headship is "sound doctrine," yet it is abrasive to the modern mind. Consequently, congregations gather teachers who will soften the blow. They seek leaders who will reinterpret submission as mutual deference and authority as merely service. Paul warns of the result in verse 4, stating, "So they will turn their ears away from the truth and turn aside to myths." Egalitarianism is one such myth, a comforting fable that denies the biological and theological reality of creation to suit the desire for autonomy.

The Demand for Illusions

This pattern is not new. The second witness, Isaiah 30:10, records the demand of a rebellious people who say, "Do not prophesy to us the truth! Speak to us pleasant words; prophesy illusions."

A church that refuses to teach the hierarchy of the home is prophesying an illusion. It presents a world where authority is unnecessary and roles are fluid. This offers "pleasant words" to a culture at war with the Father, but it hides the coming judgment. When the church validates the culture's rebellion, it ceases to be the pillar and foundation of the truth. It becomes a mirror reflecting the world's errors back to it, blessed with religious language.

The Judgment of Inversion

The silence of the pulpit leads inevitably to the inversion of society. When men fail to lead and speak truth, judgment follows in the form of role reversal. The third witness, Isaiah 3:12, laments, "Youths oppress My people, and women rule over them."

In the biblical worldview, this is not a victory for equality. It is a sign of collapse. When the church suppresses the teaching of male leadership, it does not produce strong women and humble men. It produces weak men and emboldened women who rule over them. The prophet concludes, "O My people, your guides mislead you; they turn you from your paths." By silencing the truth of hierarchy, the guides of the church are actively misleading the people, turning them from the path of order into the path of chaos.

The Watchman's Duty

The leaders who silence these truths fail in their duty as watchmen. God told Ezekiel, "Son of man, I have made you a watchman for the house of Israel. Whenever you hear a word from My mouth, give them a warning from Me" (Ezekiel 3:17).

To hear the word regarding headship and submission in Scripture but fail to speak it to the generation is a dereliction of duty. It leaves the family undefended against the ideologies that seek to destroy it. When the pulpit is silent, the pew is defenseless.

Consequences of the Silence

The result of silencing the truth is spiritual famine. Amos 8:11 warns of a time when there is "a famine of hearing the words of the LORD." When a church voluntarily stops speaking the full counsel of God to please men, God may eventually withdraw His word entirely. A church that will not preach headship will eventually not preach the gospel, for both are grounded in the authority of the Scripture and the nature of God.

We must reject the fear of man. The elders must "hold firmly to the faithful word as it was taught, so that he can encourage others by sound teaching and refute those who contradict it" (Titus 1:9). We must not offer pleasant illusions. We must offer the difficult, saving truth of God's order. When we fail to do so, we do not merely lose a theological argument. We leave the door open for specific, historical patterns of destruction to repeat themselves in our homes and churches. Scripture provides tragic portraits of what happens when this order is inverted, warning us that the cost of rebellion is always paid in ruin.

Reflection Questions

1. How does the warning in 2 Timothy 4:3 about "itching ears" explain the modern church's popularity of egalitarian teachers?
2. In light of Isaiah 30:10, how is the message of "mutual submission" (when used to deny headship) an example of "pleasant words" and "illusions"?
3. Why is the pastor's role as a "watchman" (Ezekiel 3:17) critical in the cultural battle over male/female roles?

> ***On Courage:*** *"It costs nothing to preach what the culture applauds. The test of a faithful teacher is whether he will say what God says when the world, and the church, is screaming for him to stop."*
>
> ***On Silence:*** *"Silence is not neutral. When the Bible speaks clearly and the pulpit stays quiet, the silence is a lie. It tells the people that God does not care about how they order their lives."*

8.3 - Negative Biblical Examples

Ahab/Jezebel, Samson/Delilah, Ananias/Sapphira Scripture provides stark negative examples where female usurpation of male authority and male abdication of responsibility bring ruin and judgment. These narratives confirm the dangers of inverting God's design, demonstrating that whether in marriage or outside of it, when a man yields his strength to a woman's control, it leads to spiritual and physical death.

🕮 THE WITNESSES

I. **1 Kings 21**
25: "Surely there was never one like Ahab, who sold himself to do evil in the sight of the LORD, incited by his wife Jezebel."

II. **Judges 16**
16: "Finally, after she had pressed him daily with her words and pleaded until he was sick to death,"

III. **Acts 5**
2: "With his wife's full knowledge, he kept back some of the proceeds for himself, but brought a portion and laid it at the apostles' feet."

These tragic narratives confirm the dangers warned against in Chapter 8.2 and illustrate the inversion of the Father's Chain of Headship set forth in Chapter 2.1.

Ahab and Jezebel: The Archetype of Inversion

The narrative of Ahab and Jezebel stands as the ultimate biblical warning against the inversion of marital roles. Ahab, the king of

Israel, consistently abdicated his moral and spiritual leadership, while Jezebel, his wife, usurped authority to lead the nation into idolatry and bloodshed.

The Mechanism of Incitement

Ahab's failure was not merely that he sinned, but that he submitted to the direction of his wife in doing so. The primary witness states, "Surely there was never one like Ahab, who sold himself to do evil in the sight of the LORD, incited by his wife Jezebel" (1 Kings 21:25).

The Hebrew word for "incited" implies stirring up or driving. Ahab was the king, holding the office of authority, but Jezebel was the driving force. This dynamic mirrors the Fall in Genesis, where Adam listened to the voice of his wife over the command of God. When a man abdicates his position as head, he creates a vacuum that is often filled by unrighteous usurpation. Ahab functioned as the passive beneficiary of his wife's ruthless strength, but Scripture holds him accountable for the evil she committed in his name.

Usurpation of the Seal

When Ahab sulked because he could not acquire Naboth's vineyard, Jezebel took the reins of leadership. She mocked his passivity, asking in 1 Kings 21:7, "Do you not reign over Israel?" She then wrote letters in Ahab's name and sealed them with his seal to orchestrate a murder. She used his authority to execute her will. The result was judgment upon the entire house of Ahab. The curse of Isaiah 3:12 was fully realized in their reign, for a woman ruled over him, leading the people into destruction.

Samson and Delilah: Strength Surrendered to Seduction

The case of Samson and Delilah offers a distinct warning. Unlike Ahab, Samson was not married to Delilah. She was a woman of the Valley of Sorek, likely a Philistine, whom he "loved" (Judges 16:4). This narrative demonstrates that the danger of inversion exists even outside the covenant of marriage. When a man yields his God-given strength to please a woman, regardless of their status, he forfeits his power.

The Tyranny of Emotional Pressure

Delilah's weapon was not physical force but persistent emotional manipulation. The second witness records, "Finally, after she had pressed him daily with her words and pleaded until he was sick to death" (Judges 16:16). Samson, who could tear a lion apart with his bare hands, could not withstand the pressure of a woman who refused to submit to his silence. He prioritized relational peace over his consecration to God.

The Cost of Disorder

Because Samson submitted to Delilah's demand rather than ruling over his own spirit, he lost his vision and his freedom. Judges 16:21 tells us the Philistines "seized him, gouged out his eyes, and brought him down to Gaza." The visual nature of his judgment is significant. He followed the desire of his eyes rather than the law of God, and he allowed a woman to master him. Inversion led to blindness. A man who cannot say "no" to a woman will eventually say "no" to God.

Ananias and Sapphira: The Headship of Accountability

In the New Testament, the case of Ananias and Sapphira reveals that even in a mutual conspiracy, the husband bears the primary weight of leadership and accountability before God.

Shared Guilt, Ordered Judgment

The third witness, Acts 5:2, states that Ananias acted "with his wife's full knowledge." They agreed together to lie to the Holy Spirit. However, when judgment fell, Peter confronted Ananias first.

Acts 5:3 records Peter's question: "Ananias, how is it that Satan has filled your heart to lie to the Holy Spirit...?" Ananias fell down and died immediately. It was only "about three hours later" (Acts 5:7) that his wife came in, unaware of what had happened. She confirmed the lie and also died.

No Excuse in Mutuality

While Sapphira was fully complicit and personally accountable for her sin, the sequence of judgment highlights the principle of headship. Ananias cannot blame his wife, nor can he claim "mutual agreement" as a shield. As the head, he is responsible for the spiritual direction of his home. He failed to protect his wife from sin; instead, he led her into it. The lesson is clear. A husband is accountable for the culture of his household. If he leads his wife into error, or passively allows her to join him in error, he bears the primary weight of the judgment.

The Heavy Cost of Reversed Roles

These three narratives provide a sobering composite of inversion.

1. **Ahab** shows us the **passive husband** who allows his wife to drive him to evil, resulting in the destruction of his dynasty.
2. **Samson** shows us the **undisciplined man** who yields his strength to female emotional manipulation, resulting in the loss of his power and vision.
3. **Ananias** shows us the **conspiring husband** who fails to lead in truth, resulting in immediate judgment on the family unit.

In all three cases, the man failed to exercise godly headship. He failed to rule, to protect, and to lead. The result was not a partnership of equals, but a disaster of disobedience. God's order is not a suggestion for a specific cultural epoch. It is a safeguard.

When it is removed, the family and the nation are left exposed to the enemy.

This failure of leadership in the home often drifts into the church. As we transition to the next chapter, we will examine how the blurring of roles has moved from the private sphere to the public platform, specifically regarding the distinction between prophecy and authoritative teaching.

Reflection Questions

1. How does the description of Ahab being "incited" by Jezebel (1 Kings 21:25) illustrate the spiritual danger of a passive husband?
2. Samson was not married to Delilah, yet he yielded to her. What does this teach men about the danger of surrendering their strength to gain female approval?
3. Why is it significant that Peter confronted Ananias first (Acts 5:3), even though the text says they acted with full mutual knowledge?

> ***On Influence:*** *"Ahab had the crown, but Jezebel had the control. A man who refuses to rule his own house will eventually find his house ruling him."*
>
> ***On Strength:*** *"Samson proved that physical strength is useless without spiritual backbone. He could kill a thousand men, but he couldn't handle one woman's nagging. That was his defeat."*

8.4 - Prophecy vs Teaching in Modern Ministry

Conferences, Podcasts, and Platforms Building on the apostolic distinction between prophecy and teaching rigorously established in Chapter 6.2, this chapter applies that line to contemporary platforms and ministries.

Modern ministries often confuse the gift of prophecy with the office of teaching, leading to the unauthorized elevation of women in the pulpit and on digital platforms. Scripture distinguishes these functions. Prophecy is for edification and is permitted to women under authority, whereas authoritative teaching of doctrine is restricted to men. Maintaining this distinction prevents the inversion of the sexes in the public assembly and media.

🕮 THE WITNESSES

I. **1 Timothy 2**
12: "I do not permit a woman to teach or to exercise authority over a man; she is to remain quiet."

II. **1 Corinthians 14**
34: "Women are to be silent in the churches. They are not permitted to speak, but must be in submission, as the law says."

III. **1 Corinthians 14**
3: "But he who prophesies speaks to men for their edification, encouragement, and comfort."

The Distinction Between Prophecy and Teaching

To navigate the landscape of modern ministry, we must first define our terms biblically. Egalitarians often argue that because women prophesied in the Bible, they should be allowed to preach and teach doctrine today. This argument collapses when we examine the distinct definitions and limitations Scripture places on these two activities.

Teaching: The Authoritative Deposit

The prohibition in the primary witness is specific. Paul writes, "I do not permit a woman to teach or to exercise authority over a man" (1 Timothy 2:12). The word for "teach" (*didaskō*) in the pastoral epistles refers to the preservation and authoritative transmission of the apostolic deposit. It is the defining of doctrine and the instruction of the conscience. This function is inextricably linked to exercising authority (*authentein*). It is the role of the father in the home and the elder in the church. It is restricted to the male sex by creation design, as Paul establishes in 1 Timothy 2:13.

Prophecy: Edification Under Authority

Prophecy is distinct from teaching. The third witness defines its scope: "But he who prophesies speaks to men for their edification, encouragement, and comfort" (1 Corinthians 14:3). Prophecy appeals to the will and heart based on revealed truth, but it does not establish doctrine. Furthermore, New Testament prophecy is not infallible; it is subject to judgment by the leadership. 1 Corinthians 14:29 commands, "Two or three prophets should speak, and the others should weigh carefully what is said."

Because prophecy is for edification and is subject to male headship, women were permitted to exercise this gift, provided they displayed a sign of authority. 1 Corinthians 11:5 mentions "every woman who prays or prophesies," indicating active participation. However, this participation never crossed the line into authoritative teaching or governance. The woman could speak to edify, but she could not speak to rule or define doctrine.

The Violation in Modern Platforms

The digital age has created a new venue for the violation of this order. The "platform," whether a conference stage, a podcast, or a video channel, often functions as a pulpit.

The Conference Circuit

When a woman stands behind a pulpit or on a conference stage to open the Bible and instruct a mixed audience of men and women in the meaning of the text, she is functioning as a teacher. She is exercising authority over the men in the audience by directing their understanding of Scripture. This is a direct violation of 1 Timothy 2:12. It matters not if she calls it "sharing" or if she is under the "covering" of a pastor. If the act itself is teaching doctrine to men, it is prohibited. The medium does not nullify the mandate.

Precision Regarding "Co-Preaching"

A common trend in modern churches is the husband-wife teaching team, often called "co-preaching." Proponents argue that because the husband is present, the wife is under authority and therefore not violating Scripture. This argument fails to distinguish between *being under authority* and *exercising the function of a man.*

1 Timothy 2:12 does not say, "I do not permit a woman to teach alone." It says, "I do not permit a woman to teach... over a man." The presence of the husband does not change the nature of the act. If the wife is expounding Scripture and instructing the men in the congregation on doctrine, she is teaching.

The biblical precedent often cited for this is Priscilla and Aquila. However, Acts 18:26 states that they "took him aside and explained to him the way of God more accurately." This was private correction, not public preaching. Priscilla did not stand in the synagogue to instruct the assembly; she participated in a private context. Therefore, "co-preaching" where a wife instructs the gathered church violates the creation order by placing a woman in the role of authoritative instructor to men, regardless of her husband's proximity.

Podcasts and Digital Influence

The internet has allowed women to bypass the local church structure entirely. A woman who hosts a podcast teaching theology to men is exercising authority over them in the digital sphere. She is shaping their doctrine and instructing their minds. While the internet is not the local church, the principle of male headship is rooted in creation, not merely in church polity. Adam was formed first, then Eve (1 Timothy 2:13). This priority applies to the human race, not just the church meeting. Therefore, women should direct their teaching ministries toward other women, as seen in Titus 2:3-4, and children, leaving the doctrinal instruction of men to men.

The Silence of Order

The second witness, 1 Corinthians 14:34, commands women to be "silent in the churches." This silence is not absolute speechlessness, for we know they prayed and prophesied. Rather, in the context of 1 Corinthians 14, it refers to the silence of submission during the judgment of prophecy and the authoritative teaching of the word.

When the church gathers, or when the word of God is authoritatively proclaimed, the male voice is to lead. This reflects Christ's relationship to the Church. When women lead in prayer, reading, or teaching in the mixed assembly, the symbol is broken. The bride begins to speak for the Groom. We must restore the visual and auditory testimony of male leadership to our gatherings and our media.

Preserving the Distinction

The church must clarify these categories.

1. **Prophecy and Sharing:** Women may share words of encouragement, testimony, or edification, provided it is done under the oversight of male leadership and does not become doctrinal instruction.
2. **Teaching and Preaching:** The exposition of Scripture and the establishing of doctrine for the mixed assembly must be done by qualified men.

By maintaining this line, we honor the gifts God has given to women without dismantling the authority He has invested in men.

Reflection Questions

1. How does the definition of prophecy in 1 Corinthians 14:3 (edification, encouragement, comfort) differ from the authority implied in "teaching" (1 Timothy 2:12)?
2. Why does the private instruction of Apollos by Priscilla and Aquila (Acts 18:26) not justify the public practice of "co-preaching"?
3. How does the "husband-wife" preaching team undermine the biblical symbolism of Christ and the Church?

> ***On Influence:*** *"A woman teaching theology to men is not a 'culture war' issue. It is a creation issue. God designed the man to feed the flock. When the woman takes the ladle, the order is inverted."*
>
> ***On Edification:*** *"Edification is not the same as instruction. A woman can edify a man with a word of encouragement, but she cannot instruct him with a word of doctrine. The first builds up his heart; the second binds his conscience. The latter is for men."*

8.5 - Living the Divine Order

Reverential Submission and Sacrificial Love God's design for the home requires the wife to submit to her husband as an act of obedience to the Lord, and the husband to exercise headship not to please his wife, but to sanctify her. This is not a partnership of equals but a hierarchy of holiness, where the man answers to God for the spiritual direction of the woman.

This chapter articulates how the hierarchy defended in Chapters 2.1-2.3 and applied against modern distortions in 8.1-8.4 is lived out daily in the home.

🕮 THE WITNESSES

I. **Ephesians 5**
22-24: "Wives, submit to your husbands as to the Lord. For the husband is the head of the wife as Christ is the head of the church, His body, of which He is the Savior. Now as the church submits to Christ, so also wives should submit to their husbands in everything."

II. **Ephesians 5**
25-27: "Husbands, lovc your wives, just as Christ loved the church and gave Himself up for her to sanctify her, cleansing her by the washing with water through the word, and to present her to Himself as a glorious church, without stain or wrinkle or any such blemish, but holy and blameless."

III. **1 Peter 3**
5-6: "For this is how the holy women of the past adorned themselves. They put their hope in God and were submissive to their husbands, just as Sarah obeyed Abraham and called him lord. And you are her

children if you do what is right and refuse to give way to fear."

The Theology of Submission

The command for a wife to submit to her husband is absolute and theological. It is not based on the husband's competence or kindness, but on the order of creation established by God.

As to the Lord

Paul frames the command in the primary witness: "Wives, submit to your husbands as to the Lord" (Ephesians 5:22). The wife's submission to her husband is the visible expression of her submission to Christ. She cannot claim to obey God while rebelling against the head God has placed over her.

The Scope of Authority

The text establishes the scope in verse 24: "Now as the church submits to Christ, so also wives should submit to their husbands in everything." The wife does not retain a veto power. Just as the Church does not negotiate terms with Christ, the wife is called to align herself under the direction of her husband. This is not a degradation of her personhood, but a proper ordering of her function within the covenant.

The Example of Sarah

The third witness, 1 Peter 3:6, elevates Sarah as the model: "just as Sarah obeyed Abraham and called him lord." This obedience was not merely cultural etiquette; it was a recognition of his authority. Peter connects this submission directly to "hope in God" (1 Peter 3:5). A woman who trusts God proves it by submitting to the man God has assigned to her.

The Burden of Headship

The husband's role is often sentimentalized as "servant leadership" in a way that inverts the order, suggesting he exists to satisfy his wife's desires. Scripture presents headship as a heavy weight of responsibility before God.

Leadership Toward Sanctification

The husband is commanded to love his wife, but the *purpose* of that love is specific. The second witness states: "Husbands, love your wives, just as Christ loved the church and gave Himself up for her to sanctify her" (Ephesians 5:25-26).

Christ did not die to satisfy the whims of the Church; He died to make her holy. Similarly, a husband does not lead to please his wife; he leads to present her blameless before God. His love is a love of purpose. He must wash her "with water through the word" (Ephesians 5:26). This requires him to be the teacher and the standard-bearer in the home. He cannot abdicate his authority to keep the peace. True love often requires saying "no" to the wife's desires in order to say "yes" to God's requirements.

The Priority of God

The husband is the head of the wife, but "the head of every man is Christ" (1 Corinthians 11:3). The man's orientation is upward toward Christ. He receives his orders from God and implements them in his household. If he prioritizes his wife's happiness over God's law, he becomes an idolater, repeating the sin of Adam who listened to the voice of his wife (Genesis 3:17) rather than the command of God.

Ruling Well

A husband as the overseer of his home, must rule his house well (1 Timothy 3:4). This implies governance, decision-making, and the enforcement of boundaries. He is not a facilitator of consensus but the captain of the ship. His sacrificial love is demonstrated in the expenditure of his strength to protect the spiritual and physical integrity of the family unit, regardless of the cost to himself.

The Harmony of Hierarchy

When the wife submits with reverence and the husband rules with sanctifying love, the home functions according to its design. Conflict arises when this order is inverted, such as when the wife seeks control or the husband seeks to please her rather than God.

We must reject the modern egalitarian pressure to flatten these roles. The husband must carry the burden of authority; the wife must offer the gift of submission. In this distinct inequality of role, the glory of God is revealed.

However, proclaiming this truth invites hostility. As we move to the final chapter of this section, we must prepare to face the specific objections and assaults leveled against this doctrine by the culture and the compromised church.

Reflection Questions

1. How does the phrase “submit... in everything” (Ephesians 5:24) challenge the modern notion that submission is conditional or mutual?
2. In light of Ephesians 5:26, how does the husband’s duty to “sanctify” his wife distinguish biblical headship from merely “serving” her desires?
3. Why is Adam’s disobedience (Genesis 3:17) a warning to husbands who prioritize their wives’ happiness over obedience to God?

On Authority: *"A husband who refuses to rule is not being kind; he is being negligent. God gave the man authority not for his own pleasure, but for the order and protection of the home."*

On Love: *"Biblical love is not giving a woman what she wants. It is leading her toward what God commands. The husband must love God more than he loves his wife, or he will serve neither of them well."*

8.6 - Anticipating the Assault

Common Objections and Scriptural Rebuttals As the modern assault intensifies, this chapter equips believers to withstand the specific objections already previewed in 8.1, grounding male headship once more in the immutable order of creation (1 Cor 11:8-9) and the Father's Chain of Headship (2.1). The next section will move from defense to embodiment, showing how this order is lived out in the fear of God.

The modern assault on biblical hierarchy relies on cultural pressure and hermeneutical gymnastics to dismantle the plain reading of the text. However, the Scriptures provide a consistent defense. We must uphold male positional authority not as a temporary cultural fix but as a creation ordinance. We must maintain that the wife's positional inferiority in rank is fully compatible with her ontological equality in essence, just as Christ is subordinate to the Father yet fully God.

🕮 THE WITNESSES

I. **1 Timothy 2**
12-14: "I do not permit a woman to teach or to exercise authority over a man; she is to remain quiet. For Adam was formed first, and then Eve. And it was not Adam who was deceived, but the woman who was deceived and fell into transgression."

II. **1 Corinthians 11**
3: "But I want you to understand that the head of every man is Christ, and the head of the woman is man, and the head of Christ is God."

III. **Ephesians 5**
22-24: "Wives, submit to your husbands as to the

> Lord. For the husband is the head of the wife as Christ is the head of the church, His body, of which He is the Savior. Now as the church submits to Christ, so also wives should submit to their husbands in everything."

Objection 1: "Paul's Commands Were Local, Not Universal"

The Argument: A frequent objection posits that Paul's restrictions on women teaching or exercising authority (1 Timothy 2:12) were temporary instructions designed for the specific situation in Ephesus. Critics argue that uneducated women were disrupting services, or that Paul was countering the local Artemis cult. Therefore, they claim these commands do not apply to the modern church.

The Biblical Rebuttal: Paul anticipates this objection by anchoring his command in history, not local circumstances. He does not say that the women in Ephesus are uneducated. Instead, the primary witness states: "For Adam was formed first, and then Eve" (1 Timothy 2:13).

Paul appeals to the **Order of Creation** (Genesis 2) and the **Nature of the Fall** (Genesis 3). By rooting the prohibition in the formation of the first human pair, Paul establishes a universal principle. The priority of Adam's formation establishes his authority, and the deception of Eve (verse 14) serves as a perpetual warning against inverting that order. Because the reason for the rule is creation itself, the rule applies wherever the creation exists.

Objection 2: "Submission Implies Inferiority"

The Argument: This objection claims that if a wife must submit to her husband, she is inherently lesser in value, intelligence, or dignity. It equates functional subordination with ontological inferiority, arguing that equality requires identical roles.

The Biblical Rebuttal: We must distinguish between **Ontological Equality** (essence) and **Positional Inferiority** (rank). Scripture categorically rejects the idea that role distinctions imply a difference in value, yet it simultaneously affirms a strict hierarchy. The second witness provides the ultimate theological safeguard: "The head of every man is Christ, and the head of the woman is man, and the head of Christ is God" (1 Corinthians 11:3).

Christ submits to the Father, meaning He is **positionally inferior** to the Father in the order of authority. Yet, He is fully God, equal to the Father in essence and glory. If positional inferiority meant ontological inferiority, then Christ would be less than God, which is heresy. Because Christ can be positionally subordinate to the Father while remaining equal in essence, the wife can be positionally inferior to her husband in the hierarchy of the home while remaining fully his equal in humanity and dignity.

Objection 3: "Headship (Kephale) Means 'Source,' Not Authority"

The Argument: As mentioned in Chapter 8.1, egalitarian scholars often argue that the Greek word *kephale* (translated "head") should be translated as "source" (like the head of a river) rather than "authority over." They argue Paul is merely saying man is the "source" of woman (since Eve came from Adam), removing any implication of rule or obedience.

The Biblical Rebuttal: While *kephale* can carry the nuance of source, the context of the New Testament inextricably links it to authority. In the third witness, Paul parallels the husband's headship with Christ's headship over the church (Ephesians 5:23). He then commands: "Now as the church submits to Christ, so also wives should submit to their husbands in everything" (Ephesians 5:24).

The command to submit (*hupotasso*) serves as the functional response to the status of headship. Submission is owed to authority.

If *kephale* meant only "source" without authority, the command to submit would be incoherent. Furthermore, even in the "source" metaphor, the derivative is subordinate to the source. Man is the glory of God, but woman is the glory of man (1 Corinthians 11:7).

Objection 4: "Galatians 3:28 Erases Male/Female Roles"

The Argument: Critics often cite Galatians 3:28 in support of Christian egalitarianism, arguing it abolishes all role distinctions in the home and church. We've touched on this in Chapter 8.1 but since the objection is so common, its important to address in this context. The verse reads: "There is neither Jew nor Greek, slave nor free, male nor female, for you are all one in Christ Jesus."

The Biblical Rebuttal: This verse addresses **soteriological standing** (salvation), not **ecclesiastical or domestic function**. The context is justification by faith. Verse 26 explains, "You are all sons of God through faith."

Just as Jews and Greeks remain ethnically distinct, and just as Paul commanded slaves to obey masters elsewhere (Ephesians 6:5), the distinction between male and female roles remains operative. Equality in access to salvation does not negate the created order of authority. A woman is equal to a man in her standing before God, but she is commanded to submit to her husband in the order of the home. The spiritual unity of the body does not obliterate the functional structure of its members.

Objection 5: "What About Deborah?"

The Argument: The example of Deborah (Judges 4) is frequently used to prove that God endorses female leadership over men.

The Biblical Rebuttal: Deborah's judgeship serves as an indictment against a passive male generation, not a normative pattern for the church. It occurred during a time when "everyone did what was right in his own eyes" (Judges 21:25). When Barak, the military commander, refused to lead without her, Deborah prophesied: "The road you take will not lead to your glory, for the LORD will sell Sisera into the hand of a woman" (Judges 4:9).

Scripture presents female rule over men as a judgment, not a blessing. Isaiah 3:12 laments, "Youths oppress My people, and women rule over them." The New Testament standard for leadership is explicit, requiring an overseer to be "the husband of but one wife" (1 Timothy 3:2). We do not build doctrine on historical exceptions found in times of judgment; we build on the clear commands of the Apostles.

From Defense to Application

The objections to biblical hierarchy invariably collapse when tested against the whole counsel of God. The command for male headship is rooted in the unchangeable order of creation. The command for female submission is modeled on the relationship of the Son to the Father. These truths are not cultural prejudices to be discarded but divine designs to be honored.

Having established the theological foundation and refuted the modern distortions, we must now move from the theoretical to the practical. It is not enough to win an argument; we must embody the truth. In the next section, we will examine the scriptural models of how this order is lived out in the fear of God, beginning with the strength and submission of the virtuous woman.

Reflection Questions

1. How does Paul's appeal to Adam and Eve in 1 Timothy 2:13-14 refute the argument that his commands were limited to the culture of Ephesus?
2. In what way does the Trinitarian nature of God (1 Corinthians 11:3) validate the concept of "positional inferiority" without implying a lack of worth?

3. How does the context of Galatians 3:28 (justification by faith) clarify that it does not abolish functional roles in the church and home?

> ***On Context:*** *"To say Paul's commands were just for Ephesus is to say that Creation and the Fall were local events. Paul grounds his argument in Genesis, not in geography."*
>
> ***On Equality:*** *"Different roles do not mean different value. The President and the citizen are equal under the law, but they have different authority. The husband and wife are equal in grace, but distinct in authority."*

PART VI: SCRIPTURAL MODELS AND PRACTICAL OBEDIENCE

Chapter 9: Living the Order – Biblical Models

9.1 - Proverbs 31: Strength in Submission

The Proverbs 31 woman is not a model of the modern career woman but the ultimate example of the *ezer kenegdo* functioning in perfect order. Her extraordinary strength and industry are not independent of her husband but are the very means by which she submits to him. She serves him as a duty derived from her creation, employing her capability to secure his dominion and glory.

This chapter exegetes Proverbs 31 to demonstrate how the virtuous woman's industry fulfills, rather than contradicts, the subordinate role established in the Father's Chain of Headship (2.1) and defended throughout this book.

🕮 THE WITNESSES

I. **Proverbs 31**
   11-12: "The heart of her husband trusts in her, and he lacks nothing of value. She brings him good and not harm all the days of her life."
II. **Proverbs 31**
   23: "Her husband is known at the city gates, where he sits among the elders of the land."
III. **1 Peter 3**
   5-6: "For this is how the holy women of the past adorned themselves. They put their hope in God and were submissive to their husbands, just as Sarah obeyed Abraham and called him lord. And you are her children if you do what is right and refuse to give way to fear."

The Myth of Independent Power

In modern church culture, the Proverbs 31 woman is often presented as a feminist icon wrapped in biblical clothing. Commentators focus extensively on her real estate dealings, her manufacturing, and her financial acumen to argue that biblical womanhood is indistinguishable from the modern career woman. This interpretation suggests that her value lies in her autonomy and her ability to function without male oversight. It appeals to a culture that views submission as weakness and dependence as a liability.

But this view severs the text from its context. The Bible does not present the excellent wife as an independent agent operating in a vacuum. Her strength is not autonomous. It is derived and directed. To read Proverbs 31 as a manifesto for female independence is to ignore the hierarchy of the passage. Her labor is not for her own name but for her husband's. She is powerful precisely because she is under authority.

Excellence within the Order

Scripture presents the Proverbs 31 woman as the ultimate *ezer kenegdo* (helper suitable). Her industry is massive, but it is framed entirely by her positional subordination to her head.

1. The Foundation of Trust The text opens by establishing her relationship to authority. Proverbs 31:11 states, "The heart of her husband trusts in her, and he lacks nothing of value." This trust is not the result of her independence but of her absolute reliability as his subordinate. She is not competing with him. She is completing him. Her freedom to buy fields and plant vineyards exists only because her husband has authorized her stewardship over his resources. She acts as his deputy, not his partner.

2. Elevating the Head Her hard work has a specific directional purpose: the glory of her husband. Proverbs 31:23 declares, "Her husband is known at the city gates, where he sits among the elders of the land." Her domestic management and economic success do not build her own platform. They secure his reputation and standing in the community. This mirrors the church's role in glorifying Christ. As Paul writes in 1 Corinthians 11:7, "the woman is the glory of man." Her excellence makes him shine. If she becomes the focus, the order is inverted.

3. Strength for the Task Her submission is not passivity. The text says, "She girds herself with strength and shows that her arms are strong" (Proverbs 31:17). She buys fields, plants vineyards, and trades profitably. Yet this strength is exercised for the household under the covering of her husband. She exemplifies the teaching of Titus 2:5 to be "busy at home... and subject to their own husbands, so that the word of God will not be discredited." Her competence silences the critics of God's order by proving that submission produces the highest form of productivity.

The Gentle Spirit of Sarah

The New Testament confirms that this type of strength is rooted in submission. Peter points to the "holy women of the past" as the model for Christian wives. He writes in 1 Peter 3:5-6, "For this is how the holy women of the past adorned themselves. They put their hope in God and were submissive to their husbands, just as Sarah obeyed Abraham and called him lord."

1. True Adornment Peter clarifies that a woman's true strength is not external show but internal character. It is "the unfading beauty of a gentle and quiet spirit, which is precious in God's sight." (1 Peter 3:4). The Proverbs 31 woman possesses this spirit. She does not nag or contend. She works willingly with her hands and speaks with wisdom. Her industry is an expression of her quiet confidence in her assigned role.

2. Fear of the Lord The secret to her submissive strength is revealed in the poem's conclusion. Proverbs 31:30 states, "Charm is deceptive and beauty is fleeting, but a woman who fears the LORD is to be praised." Her submission to her husband is an overflow of her fear of God. She submits "as to the Lord" (Ephesians 5:22), recognizing that honoring her husband's headship is her primary duty to her Creator. She fears God too much to dishonor the head He has placed over her.

A Warrior in the Garden

The Proverbs 31 woman is a warrior in a garden, a powerhouse of industry, and a pillar of strength. Yet she is all of these things precisely because she is not rebellious. She is a submissive helper whose competence allows her husband to sit at the city gates with confidence. This is the biblical model: distinct roles, unified purpose, and powerful hierarchy. When a woman embraces this order, she becomes a force for good that no modern definition of empowerment can rival.

Reflection Questions

1. How does Proverbs 31:23 demonstrate that a wife's primary ministry is the elevation of her husband's standing rather than her own?
2. In what ways does modern culture try to detach the virtuous woman's industry from her submission, and why is this dangerous?
3. How does the example of Sarah calling Abraham "lord" (1 Peter 3:6) inform our understanding of the "fear of the Lord" in Proverbs 31:30?

> ***On Competence:*** *"The virtuous woman's capability is not a license for autonomy. She does not build a career; she builds her husband's house. Her industry is the direct application of her submission, deploying all her strength to magnify his headship."*
>
> ***On Purpose:*** *"A wife's success is measured by her husband's reputation at the city gates. If she is famous but he is forgotten, the order is inverted. She is the glory of the man, not the glory of herself."*

9.2 - Titus 2: Older Women Training the Younger

Titus 2 establishes a clear mandate for intergenerational discipleship among women. While Scripture restricts women from teaching doctrine to men, it explicitly commands older women to train younger women. This training is not focused on career advancement or self-actualization but on the practical application of submission, domestic management, and love for the family. The ultimate goal of this instruction is the preservation of the integrity of the Word of God.

This mandate for older women to train younger women in domestic obedience and submission directly applies the hierarchical order set forth in Chapters 2.1 and 8.5, protecting the reputation of the Gospel in the household.

🕮 THE WITNESSES

I. **Titus 2**
   3-5: "Older women, likewise, are to be reverent in their behavior, not slanderers or addicted to much wine, but teachers of good. In this way they can train the young women to love their husbands and children, to be self-controlled, pure, managers of their households, kind, and submissive to their own husbands, so that the word of God will not be discredited."

II. **1 Timothy 5**
   14: "So I advise the younger widows to marry, have children, and manage their households, denying the adversary occasion for slander."

III. **1 Timothy 2**

12: "I do not permit a woman to teach or to exercise authority over a man; she is to remain quiet."

The Mandate of Mentorship

Scripture assigns a vital, specific role to older women in the church. While they are restricted from teaching doctrine to men or exercising authority over them (1 Timothy 2:12), they are explicitly commanded to teach and train younger women. This training is not abstract theology but practical godliness centered on the domestic sphere and the preservation of the divine order. It serves as the transmission mechanism for biblical womanhood from one generation to the next.

Older Women: Qualifications and Role

Paul begins by establishing the character requirements for this ministry. He instructs: "Older women likewise are to be reverent in their behavior, not slanderers or addicted to much wine, but teachers of good" (Titus 2:3). Before they can train others, they must embody the truth. Reverence must mark their conduct. They must have conquered the vices of the tongue (slander) and the flesh (addiction). Only then are they qualified to be "teachers of good." This "good" is defined in the subsequent verses as the practical application of God's order in the home.

Core Training for Younger Women

The curriculum for younger women is specific and centered on the household. Paul writes: "In this way they can train the younger women to love their husbands and children, to be self-controlled, pure, managers of their households, kind, and submissive to their own husbands" (Titus 2:4-5).

1. Domestic Affection The training begins with the heart of the home. They are to be trained to be *philandros* (lovers of husbands) and *philoteknos* (lovers of children). This love is not merely sentimental but involves the devoted service required to build a home and support the headship of the husband.

2. Domestic Management The BSB translates the Greek term *oikourgos* as "managers of their households." This defines the wife's primary sphere of influence and labor. She is to be the guardian and administrator of the home under her husband's authority. This parallels Paul's instruction in 1 Timothy 5:14, where he advises younger widows to "marry, have children, and manage their households." The home is not a place of confinement but of active management and stewardship. It is the base of operation for the dominion mandate.

3. Submission The list culminates in the command to be "submissive to their own husbands" (Titus 2:5). The older women must teach the younger women that submission is a virtue, not a vice. This aligns perfectly with Ephesians 5:22-24, which establishes the husband as the head of the wife. It is notable that this must be *taught* and *trained*. The sinful nature desires to rule over the husband (Genesis 3:16); therefore, the older women must train the younger to conquer this impulse and submit.

The Purpose: Protecting the Word

Paul provides the theological reason for this rigorous adherence to domestic order: "so that the word of God will not be discredited" (Titus 2:5). When Christian women reject their God-assigned roles, neglect their homes, or rebel against their husbands, it gives the enemies of God occasion to blaspheme. Conversely, when women live out this order, they adorn the gospel.

This principle is confirmed in 1 Timothy 6:1, where servants are told to honor their masters "so that God's name and our teaching will not be discredited." Submission protects the reputation of the faith. A rebellious wife is a walking contradiction to the gospel of a submissive Christ.

The Challenge of the Hard Case

The instruction in Titus 2 assumes the norm of Christian marriage. It creates a multi-generational reinforcement of God's hierarchy. Older women, having lived the struggle and the blessing of submission, are to mentor the younger generation. They teach that strength is found in order, not autonomy. By loving their husbands, managing their homes, and submitting to authority, women silence the adversary and glorify their Creator.

However, the question often arises: What if the husband is not worthy of such honor? What if he is foolish or harsh? Does the command to submit still apply? To answer this, we must look to the scriptural example of a woman who navigated this precise difficulty with wisdom and grace. In the next chapter, we will examine the life of Abigail.

Reflection Questions

1. How does the list of virtues in Titus 2:4-5 culminate in the command to submit, and why is this significant for the reputation of the church?
2. Why is the teaching ministry of older women limited to younger women and children, according to the context of 1 Timothy 2:12?
3. How does the mismanagement of the household or rebellion against a husband "discredit" the Word of God?

> ***On Priority:*** *"The church does not need more women preachers; it needs more women who love their husbands and manage their homes. The former is a violation of Scripture; the latter is the fulfillment of it."*
>
> ***On Testimony:*** *"A wife's rebellion is not just a marital issue; it is a gospel issue. When she refuses to submit, she hands the enemies of God a weapon to attack the Word."*

9.3 - Abigail: Wisdom in Submission

Abigail stands as the biblical corrective to the false notion that submission requires a wife to follow a foolish husband into destruction. Her decisive intervention in 1 Samuel 25 demonstrates that the *ezer* is a warrior who fights for her household. She honors the structure of authority by preventing bloodshed and preserving her husband's life, proving that true submission is an active, discerning exercise of wisdom that aligns with God's ultimate order.

Abigail stands as the biblical corrective to the false notion that submission requires blind passivity, showing how an *ezer* can exercise strength and discernment while honoring the structure of authority defended in 8.5 and 2.1.

🕮 THE WITNESSES

I. **1 Samuel 25**
3: "His name was Nabal, and his wife's name was Abigail. She was an intelligent and beautiful woman, but her husband, a Calebite, was harsh and evil in his dealings."

II. **1 Samuel 25**
23-24: "When Abigail saw David, she quickly got off the donkey, fell facedown, and bowed before him. She fell at his feet and said, 'My lord, may the blame be on me alone, but please let your servant speak to you; hear the words of your servant.'"

III. **1 Samuel 25**
32-33: "Then David said to Abigail, 'Blessed be the LORD, the God of Israel, who sent you to meet me this day! Blessed is your discernment, and blessed are you,

> because today you kept me from bloodshed and from avenging myself by my own hand.'"

The Dilemma of the Foolish Head

The doctrine of headship often faces its most severe test in the "hard case." What is a Christian wife to do when her husband acts not merely with incompetence, but with wicked folly that endangers the entire family? The Scriptures do not leave us without an answer. The narrative of Nabal and Abigail provides a divine case study on how a wife navigates the failure of her head without becoming a rebel herself.

Nabal is described as "harsh and evil in his dealings" (1 Samuel 25:3). When David, the anointed king of Israel, sent messengers to request food in return for the protection his men had provided to Nabal's flocks, Nabal insulted them and refused. His refusal was not just stinginess; it was a violation of hospitality and a provocation of war. David swore to kill every male belonging to Nabal by morning (1 Samuel 25:22).

This scenario presents the critical distinction between **positional submission** and **moral complicity**. Abigail did not join her husband in his folly, nor did she sit passively while destruction approached. She recognized that her primary duty as an *ezer* was to preserve the life of the household entrusted to her care.

Wise Intervention Without Usurpation

Upon hearing of the danger from a servant, Abigail did not convene a committee or argue with her husband, who was likely drunk. Instead, she acted within her domain as the steward of the household to preserve it.

1. Swift Execution of Duty The text records her competence in 1 Samuel 25:18: "Then Abigail hurried and took two hundred loaves of bread, two skins of wine, five butchered sheep, five seahs of roasted grain, a hundred clusters of raisins, and two hundred cakes of figs." She did not ask permission to save her husband's life. She acted on the necessity of the moment to fulfill her duty as a faithful helper. She used the resources of the household to save the head of the household.

2. The Posture of Intercession When she met David, she did not come as a rebel denouncing her husband, but as a humble intercessor. The second witness records that she "fell facedown, and bowed before him" (1 Samuel 25:23). She took the guilt upon herself, saying, "My lord, may the blame be on me alone" (1 Samuel 25:24). By absorbing the guilt, she diffused the king's anger. She acted as a shield for her husband, placing herself between him and the sword of David.

3. Appealing to Higher Authority Abigail appealed to David's true identity and his obligation to God. She reminded him that he fought the battles of the LORD and that he should not have bloodguilt on his hands when he became ruler over Israel (1 Samuel 25:28-31). She acknowledged Nabal's nature honestly, stating, "His name means Fool, and folly accompanies him" (1 Samuel 25:25), yet she did so to save him, not to mock him. She aligned herself with the anointed King to save her present lord.

David's Blessing and God's Order

David recognized that Abigail's intervention was of the Lord. He declared in the third witness: "Blessed be the LORD, the God of Israel, who sent you to meet me this day! Blessed is your discernment" (1 Samuel 25:32-33).

By listening to her, David was restrained from sinning. Abigail's submission to God's law regarding bloodshed helped David maintain his own alignment with God. She did not emasculate David or Nabal; she prevented David from destroying his own reputation and Nabal from dying prematurely by the sword.

The outcome confirms the righteousness of her action. She returned home and found Nabal drunk. She waited until morning to tell him what she had done. When she told him, "his heart failed within him, and he became like a stone" (1 Samuel 25:37). Ten days later, the LORD struck Nabal and he died (1 Samuel 25:38). Because she honored the order even under a wicked husband, God vindicated her and placed her under a righteous head, as David took her as his wife.

The Ezer as a Wall of Defense

Abigail demonstrates that a woman's wisdom is a wall of defense for her house. She did not usurp her husband's authority. She compensated for his lack of it to save the family entrusted to him. She acted with discretion, humility, and speed. Her strength was not in rebellion, but in a discerning submission that recognized the higher law of God while maintaining respect for the structures of authority.

However, not all women act with such wisdom. Scripture also provides the contrasting example of a woman who usurped authority, led her husband into sin, and brought judgment upon a nation. In the next chapter, we will examine the spirit of rebellion through the life of Jezebel.

Reflection Questions

1. How does Abigail's humility in 1 Samuel 25:23-24 demonstrate strength rather than weakness?
2. Why did David credit Abigail's "discernment" with saving him from sin (1 Samuel 25:33), and what does this teach men about listening to a wise wife?
3. How does Abigail's action differ from the rebellion of Jezebel or the deception of Eve?

> ***On Crisis:*** *"Submission is not a suicide pact. When a husband's folly endangers the family, the godly wife acts like Abigail; not to destroy him, but to save the household he threatens."*
>
> ***On Influence:*** *"A woman's greatest power is not found in demanding rights, but in the discerning use of influence. Abigail saved her house with bread and wisdom; Jezebel destroyed hers with paint and commands."*

9.4 - Rebellion's Folly

Rebellion Leads to Judgment Rebellion against the divinely established order of headship invites inevitable judgment. While Abigail demonstrates the wisdom of an *ezer* saving her household through discerning submission, Scripture provides stark warnings of the opposite spirit. Through Jezebel, Miriam, and Michal, the Bible exposes the three faces of rebellion: usurpation of authority, the demand for egalitarian status, and contempt for the head. In every case the result is not liberation but destruction, shame, and barrenness.

While Abigail demonstrates the wisdom of submission under authority (9.3), this chapter contrasts her with the destructive rebellion of Jezebel, Miriam, and Michal, confirming the warnings of judgment for inversion given in 8.3.

🕮 THE WITNESSES

I. **1 Kings 21**
25: "Surely there was never one like Ahab, who sold himself to do evil in the sight of the Lord, incited by his wife Jezebel."

II. **Numbers 12**
2: "'Does the LORD speak only through Moses?' they said. 'Does He not also speak through us?' And the LORD heard this."

III. **2 Samuel 6**
23: "And Michal the daughter of Saul had no children to the day of her death."

The Spirit of Usurpation: Jezebel

In Chapter 8.3 we examined the mechanics of inversion through the failure of Ahab. Here we must address the spirit of the woman who filled that void. Jezebel stands as the dark inversion of the biblical wife. While Abigail interceded to prevent bloodshed and save her house (Chapter 9.3), Jezebel usurped authority to shed innocent blood and destroyed her house.

1. The Incitement to Evil The primary witness states that Ahab "sold himself to do evil" because he was "incited by his wife Jezebel" (1 Kings 21:25). The Hebrew conveys the idea of inciting or stirring up. Rather than being a helper who influences her husband toward righteousness, she was a driver who steered him toward destruction. A wife's influence is powerful. When disconnected from the fear of God it becomes a lethal weapon.

2. Seizing the Scepter When Ahab sulked because he could not buy Naboth's vineyard, he failed to lead. Jezebel stepped into the vacuum and declared, "I will get you the vineyard" (1 Kings 21:7). She wrote letters in Ahab's name and sealed them with his seal. This is the definition of usurpation. She took the symbols of his authority to execute her own will. The result was not the strengthening of the kingdom but the pronouncement of doom upon the entire house of Ahab. Usurpation does not build the house; it tears it down.

The Error of Egalitarianism: Miriam

While Jezebel represents open tyranny, Miriam represents the subtle rebellion of religious egalitarianism. Miriam was a prophetess and a leader in Israel (Micah 6:4). Yet her spiritual gifting became a stumbling block when she used it to challenge the positional authority of Moses.

1. The Claim of Equality In Numbers 12:2, Miriam and Aaron asked, "Does the LORD speak only through Moses?... Does He not also speak through us?" This is the core argument of modern egalitarianism. The logic posits that because a woman possesses spiritual gifts or hears from God, she has a right to equal authority with the man God has placed in position. Miriam confused her *function* as a prophetess with Moses' *office* as the head of the house of Israel.

2. The Divine Rebuttal God's response was immediate and severe. He summoned them and clarified that while He speaks to prophets in dreams, His relationship with Moses was unique. He then asked, "Why then were you unafraid to speak against My servant Moses?" (Numbers 12:8). The issue was not gifting. The issue was order.

3. The Shame of Rebellion When the cloud lifted, "suddenly Miriam became leprous, white as snow" (Numbers 12:10). It is significant that only Miriam was struck, though Aaron was also involved. As the instigator of the challenge to male headship, she bore the mark of judgment. Her punishment was compared to as "if her father had but spit in her face" (Numbers 12:14). She was shut out of the camp for seven days, halting the progress of the entire nation. Rebellion against God's order brings shame and hinders the advancement of God's people.

The Spirit of Contempt: Michal

The third form of rebellion is found in the heart of Michal, the daughter of Saul and wife of David. Her rebellion was not a grab for power but an internal posture of contempt for her husband.

1. Despising the Head When David danced before the Ark of the Covenant with all his might, Michal watched from a window. 2 Samuel 6:16 records that "she despised him in her heart." She judged his spiritual expression by her own standards of dignity and decorum. She placed herself above her head in judgment and mocked him when he returned to bless his household (2 Samuel 6:20).

2. The Curse of Barrenness The consequence of her contempt is recorded with chilling finality: "And Michal the daughter of Saul had no children to the day of her death" (2 Samuel 6:23). Whether this was a divine closing of the womb or the result of David withdrawing intimacy, the theological lesson is clear. Contempt for one's husband may lead to fruitlessness. A wife who mocks her head cuts off the flow of life in her marriage and her legacy.

The Fruit of Disorder

The narratives of Jezebel, Miriam, and Michal serve as divine guardrails. They warn us that strength without submission is destructive. Jezebel proves that a woman who rules her husband destroys her house. Miriam proves that spiritual gifting is not a license to challenge authority. Michal proves that contempt leads to barrenness. The biblical woman avoids these paths of destruction. She chooses instead the path of Sarah and Abigail: strength under control, used to build, preserve, and glorify.

However, the command to submit is not merely for the easy days. The true test of faith arises when authority is difficult, harsh, or unreasonable. How does a believer maintain the order of God when the leader is unworthy? In the final chapter of this section, we will examine **Practical Obedience Under Fire**, applying these principles to the workplace, the church, and the home.

Reflection Questions

1. How does the story of Jezebel demonstrate that a wife's influence, when not submitted to God's law, becomes a destructive force?
2. In what ways does the modern church repeat the error of Miriam by using "spiritual gifts" to justify bypassing the order of headship?
3. What is the connection between Michal's contempt for David and her subsequent barrenness, and how does this apply to marriage today?

On Usurpation: *"Jezebel did not want a partner; she wanted a puppet. When a woman takes the wheel, she drives the family off a cliff. God will not bless the inversion of His order."*

On Gifting: *"Miriam was a prophetess, but she was not the head. Spiritual gifts are given to serve the body, not to decapitate the head. Equality of essence does not grant equality of authority."*

9.5 - Practical Obedience Under Fire

Work, Church, Family Biblical hierarchy is not contingent upon the kindness or competence of the leader. In work, church, and family, the believer is commanded to submit to authority figures even when they are "unreasonable" (*skolios*). However, this submission is not absolute; it is bounded by the higher law of God. The Christian submits to the office to honor God but refuses to sin to obey God. This refusal is not an act of egalitarian rebellion but an act of higher loyalty to the Supreme Head.

This chapter applies the doctrine of hierarchy, established in the Father's Chain of Headship (2.1) and lived out in the virtuous examples of Chapters 9.1-9.4, to hostile environments in work, church, and family.

🕮 THE WITNESSES

I. **1 Peter 2**
18-19: "Servants, submit yourselves to your masters with all respect, not only to those who are good and gentle, but even to those who are unreasonable. For if anyone endures the pain of unjust suffering because he is conscious of God, this is to be commended."

II. **Ephesians 6**
5-7: "Slaves, obey your earthly masters with respect and fear and sincerity of heart, just as you would obey Christ. And do this not only to please them while they are watching, but as servants of Christ, doing the will of God from your heart. Serve with good will, as to the Lord and not to men,"

III. **Acts 5**

29: "But Peter and the other apostles replied, 'We must obey God rather than men.'"

Hierarchy in a Hostile World

It is easy to affirm hierarchy when the authority is benevolent and the commands are just. The true test of the "Forgotten Order" arises when the authority is harsh, incompetent, or hostile to the truth. A critical distinction must be made between **submission to the office** and **compliance with sin**. Biblical submission is not absolute obedience to human will; it is absolute obedience to God, which necessitates a respectful posture toward the human authorities He has established. We submit to the man for the Lord's sake, but we never submit to sin for the man's sake.

Work: The Unreasonable Master

The workplace often presents the challenge of the difficult boss. The Greek term used in the primary witness (1 Peter 2:18) is *skolios*, translated as "unreasonable" or "crooked." This refers to a leader who is unfair, harsh, or morally twisted.

1. Submission to Character vs. Command Peter instructs servants to submit "with all respect" even to the crooked master. The believer does not have the right to rebel simply because the boss is unkind or demanding. We honor the position because God established the structure of labor. However, this does not imply obeying a command to violate God's law. If an employer demands theft, fraud, or immorality, the believer must stand on the higher hierarchy of Ephesians 6:6, "doing the will of God." One cannot do the will of God by breaking the law of God.

2. Suffering for Good When a Christian refuses a sinful command, he may face punishment or termination. Peter frames this as "suffering for doing good" (1 Peter 3:17). This suffering is "commendable" because it demonstrates that the believer fears God more than man. We respect the boss enough not to slander him, but we respect God enough not to sin for him.

Family: Winning the Unbelieving Husband

The same principle applies in the home. 1 Peter 3:1 addresses wives whose husbands "refuse to believe the word." This creates a difficult dynamic where the head is spiritually compromised.

1. The Limit of Authority The wife is commanded to be subject to her husband so that he may be won over "without words" by her conduct. This submission involves a "pure and reverent demeanor" (1 Peter 3:2). However, authority has limits defined by God. If a husband demands his wife engage in immorality, idolatry, or fraudulent acts, she cannot comply. To do so would be to place the husband above God, which is idolatry. She must respectfully decline the sinful act while reaffirming her loyalty to his position as husband.

2. The Danger of the Egalitarian Reaction We must be careful not to use the husband's sin as an excuse to dismantle the order of the home. The modern tendency is to use the husband's failure to justify the wife's usurpation of authority. Scripture does not allow this. Even when refusing a sinful command, the wife maintains a "gentle and quiet spirit" (1 Peter 3:4). She does not fight for power; she fights for purity. Her refusal is not an act of independence but an act of obedience to Christ, her supreme Head.

Church: Order Amidst Confusion

In the church, the pressure often comes from the culture to flatten the hierarchy or from leaders who drift from Scripture.

1. Maintaining Sex Distinctions Scripture forbids women to "teach or to exercise authority over a man" (1 Timothy 2:12). This command is often attacked as culturally obsolete. However, the faithful church must maintain the distinctions of sex ordained by

God. To reject the male and female roles in the church is to reject the apostolic command.

2. The Response to False Authority If church leaders command what Scripture forbids or forbid what Scripture commands, the believer must apply the principle of Acts 5:29: "We must obey God rather than men." True submission to the Head of the Church (Christ) sometimes requires respectful dissent from earthly leaders who have abandoned His Word. We do not cause division for light causes, but we do not compromise the truth for the sake of false unity.

The Ultimate Allegiance

Practical obedience under fire requires spiritual discernment. We endure the *unreasonable behavior* of leaders to demonstrate the humility of Christ. We refuse the *sinful demands* of leaders to demonstrate the Lordship of Christ. In both actions, we glorify the God of Order. Thus the doctrine defended across this book finds its full expression in faithful obedience under fire.

This concludes our examination of the Scriptural Models. We have seen the order established in Creation, confirmed in the Chain, and lived out by the faithful. But what happens when a society, a church, or a family systematically rejects this order? The consequences are not merely theoretical; they are catastrophic. In the final section, **Part VII: Judgment and Restoration**, we will examine the inevitable chaos that follows the rejection of God's design.

Reflection Questions

1. How does 1 Peter 2:18-19 challenge the modern idea that respect must be earned before it is given?
2. In light of Acts 5:29, what are the specific biblical criteria for disobeying a human authority?

3. How can a wife refuse a sinful command from her husband without usurping his authority or displaying a rebellious spirit?

> ***On Bad Bosses:*** *"You don't submit to your boss because he is good. You submit because the LORD is good. Your work ethic is an act of worship, even if your paycheck comes from a fool."*
>
> ***On Boundaries:*** *"Submission is not complicity. If authority demands sin, rebellion against that specific command is obedience to God. But make sure it is actually sin, and not just your pride that is being offended."*

PART VII: JUDGMENT AND RESTORATION

Chapter 10: Consequences of Rejecting Hierarchy

10.1 - Societal Chaos and Fatherlessness

The systematic removal of the father from the home is not merely a sociological shift but a theological catastrophe. Scripture identifies the breakdown of the father-child bond as the precursor to a divine curse (*cherem*) that strikes the land. This judgment manifests in two distinct ways: the explosion of illegitimacy and the state-enforced stripping of paternal authority through the family court system. Both result in the captivity of the next generation and the inversion of God's created order.

🕮 THE WITNESSES

I. **Malachi 4**
   6: "And he will turn the hearts of the fathers to their children, and the hearts of the children to their fathers. Otherwise, I will come and strike the land with a curse."
II. **Isaiah 3**
   12: "Youths oppress My people, and women rule over them. O My people, your guides mislead you; they turn you from your paths."
III. **Deuteronomy 28**
   41: "You will father sons and daughters, but they will not remain yours, because they will go into captivity."

The Curse of the Severed Bond

The Old Testament closes with a haunting warning in Malachi 4:6. The final word of the English Old Testament is "curse." The Hebrew word used is *cherem*, referring to something devoted to total destruction or a ban. The condition for this destruction is the severance of the bond between fathers and children.

1. The Father as the Glory We established in Part I that the man is the glory of God and the head of the woman. By extension, the father is the glory of the children (Proverbs 17:6). When the father is removed or displaced, the glory departs (*Ichabod*). A home without a father is a home without its designated head, leaving it vulnerable to spiritual and structural collapse.

2. The Prevention of Destruction The text indicates that the restoration of patriarchal order, specifically turning hearts back to the fathers, is the only preventative measure against the land being struck with *cherem*. A society that normalizes fatherlessness is a society inviting its own annihilation.

The Landscape of Disorder: 2023 CDC Data

We need not speculate about the extent of this disorder. The breakdown of the biblical order is quantifiable. According to the *National Vital Statistics Reports* (Vol. 74, No. 1, March 18, 2025), which presents final data for 2023, the United States has normalized the severing of the father from the birth of the child.

1. The Scale of Illegitimacy In 2023, **40.0%** of all births in the United States were to unmarried women. This means that four out of every ten children entered the world without the covenant protection of a father committed to their mother and her submitted to the father by law and before God. In biblical terms, these children are born outside of "headship."

Table 10.1: Births to Unmarried Women by Origin (2023)

Maternal Group	Unmarried %
All Races	40.0%
Black	69.3%
American Indian / Alaska Native	68.7%
Hispanic	54.2%
Native Hawaiian / Other Pacific Islander	52.7%
White	26.8%
Asian	12.0%

Source: CDC National Vital Statistics Reports, Vol. 74, No. 1, Table 9.[1]

2. The State as Surrogate Husband The 2023 data confirms that when the husband is displaced, the state enters the vacuum. Medicaid was the source of payment for **41.5%** of all births in 2023. In some demographics, the reliance was even higher (64.5% for Black mothers, 58.8% for Hispanic mothers). The government effectively becomes the provider, fulfilling the role from which the father has been displaced, further entrenching the judgment.

The Inversion of Rule

Isaiah 3:12 provides a diagnostic description of a society under judgment: "Youths oppress My people, and women rule over them."

1. The Vacuum of Authority When men are removed from their station, authority does not disappear; it inverts. The text describes a scenario where the immature ("youths") become the

---

[1] National Vital Statistics Reports, Vol. 74, No. 1, March 18, 2025. * Report PDF: https://www.cdc.gov/nchs/data/nvsr/nvsr74/nvsr74-1.pdf * Total Births to Unmarried Women (40.0%): Table 9 (PDF p. 28). * Percentage by Race (Black 69.3%, White 26.8%, etc.): Table 9 (PDF p. 28). * Medicaid Source of Payment (41.5%): Table 19 (PDF p. 40).

oppressors. Without the discipline of the father, the child rules the home with tyranny.

2. The Rule of Women Isaiah lists "women rule over them" as a symptom of a collapsing state, not a sign of enlightenment. When the patriarchy falls, it is replaced not by equality, but by a matriarchal void that cannot sustain the weight of civilization. This aligns with the curse of Genesis 3:16, where the woman's desire is to control the man.

The Captivity of the Next Generation

The consequence of this disorder is foretold in the curses of the covenant. Deuteronomy 28:41 warns: "You will father sons and daughters, but they will not remain yours, because they will go into captivity."

1. State-Enforced Captivity In the modern context, this captivity manifests through the family court system and the ideology of "50/50 custody." This arrangement is often marketed as "fairness" to the parents, but biblically, it represents a fracturing of headship. A child cannot serve two masters, nor can a household have two heads with competing visions.

2. The Fracturing of Headship When the state orders a righteous father to surrender his children for half the week to a household that does not honor God, that father has been stripped of his jurisdictional authority. He retains the title of father but loses the power to command his household (Genesis 18:19). If the mother's household permits ungodly behavior, the father is legally powerless to stop it during her "time." This creates a spiritual schizophrenia in the child, who must navigate two conflicting law-systems. The state has effectively declared that the father's headship is subject to the state's permission, turning the father into a mere visitor in the life of his own offspring.

3. The Conflict of the Stepfather The issue is compounded if the mother remarries. Even if she enters a Christian home, the state-endorsed arrangement creates a profound conflict of authority. The biological father remains the *source* of the child, holding the natural right of headship by derivation. Yet, the mother still wields power over the child, and her new husband, though the head of his house, has no derivation authority over the stepchild. The biological father finds his authority legally severed for 50% of the time, while the mother retains influence throughout. This fracturing of the patrilineal line leaves the child without a single, clear head, fulfilling the curse that the children "will not remain yours."

The Harvest of Disorder

The statistics are not just numbers; they are a report card on our rejection of God's order. We have discarded the headship of the father and are reaping the whirlwind of societal chaos[2]. The solution is not more government programs or economic subsidies. The solution is the return of the hearts of the fathers to the children, and the restoration of the man to his post as the head.

But judgment does not stop at the sociological level. Scripture reveals that God's judgment often begins in the household of faith and escalates to the nations. In the next chapter, we will examine **Divine Judgment in Scripture**, tracing how God responds when His order is persistently mocked.

Reflection Questions

1. How does the "curse" in Malachi 4:6 relate to the concept of *cherem* (total destruction), and why is the father-child bond the hinge upon which this curse turns?

---

[2] **America First Policy Institute (Fatherlessness Effects):** https://www.americafirstpolicy.com/issues/issue-brief-fatherlessness-and-its-effects-on-american-society **National Center for Fathering (Statistics):** https://fathers.com/statistics-and-research/the-extent-of-fatherlessness/

2. In light of Deuteronomy 28:41, how does "50/50 custody" represent a fracturing of biblical headship and a fulfillment of the curse of captivity?
3. How does the presence of a stepfather or the mother's independent authority create a conflict with the biological father's God-given headship?

> ***On Statistics:*** *"40% of children born without a father is not a statistic; it is a suicide note written by a civilization."*
>
> ***On Custody:*** *"The 'fairness' of 50/50 custody is a lie. You cannot split headship. When you divide the authority, you destroy the order, and the children are the ones who live in the rubble."*

10.2 - Divine Judgment in Scripture

Israel, Sodom, the Church Divine judgment is not merely the natural consequence of bad choices but the active, sovereign intervention of God to protect His creation from the cancer of disorder. Scripture reveals a consistent pattern where the rejection of hierarchical and natural order necessitates a divine purge. Whether it is the earth swallowing the rebels in Israel, fire consuming the perversion of Sodom, or Christ threatening to kill the children of a seductress in the church, the Bible testifies that God defends His order with the sword of judgment.

🕮 THE WITNESSES

I. **Numbers 16**
32-33: "and the earth opened its mouth and swallowed them and their households—all Korah's men and all their possessions. They went down alive into Sheol with all they owned. The earth closed over them, and they vanished from the assembly."

II. **Genesis 19**
24: "Then the LORD rained down sulfur and fire on Sodom and Gomorrah—from the Lord out of the heavens."

III. **Revelation 2**
20-23: "But I have this against you: You tolerate that woman Jezebel, who calls herself a prophetess. By her teaching she misleads My servants to be sexually immoral and to eat food sacrificed to idols. Even though I have given her time to repent of her immorality, she is unwilling. Behold, I will cast her onto a bed of sickness, and those who commit adultery with her will suffer great tribulation unless they repent

> of her deeds. Then I will strike her children dead, and all the churches will know that I am the One who searches minds and hearts, and I will repay each of you according to your deeds."

The Judgment of Hierarchical Rebellion: Korah

The rebellion of Korah (Numbers 16) was a direct insurrection against the chain of command established by God. Korah accused Moses and Aaron of exalting themselves, arguing for a flattened hierarchy where "everyone in the entire congregation is holy" (Numbers 16:3). This was an early form of egalitarianism, denying the distinct appointment of the leader.

1. The Active Response God did not allow this disorder to resolve itself through dialogue. The response was immediate and supernatural. The text states, "the earth opened its mouth and swallowed them and their households..." (Numbers 16:32). This was a physical manifestation of a spiritual reality. Those who attempt to undermine the foundation of God's authority will be consumed by the earth they seek to rule.

2. No Tolerance for Usurpation The fire that came out from the LORD to consume the 250 men offering incense (Numbers 16:35) confirms that God views the usurpation of role as a capital offense against His holiness. The hierarchy of Israel was not a suggestion; it was the structure through which God dwelt with His people. To attack the structure was to attack the Architect.

The Judgment of Natural Chaos: Sodom

If Korah represents rebellion against authority, Sodom represents rebellion against nature. The sin of Sodom involved an aggressive inversion of the created order regarding sexuality.

1. Divine Incineration The judgment of Sodom was not a natural disaster but a targeted execution. "Then the LORD rained down burning sulfur... from the LORD out of the heavens" (Genesis 19:24). The repetition of "the LORD" emphasizes the personal agency of God in this act. He did not merely let them die; He put them to death.

2. The Severity of the Cure The destruction was total because the corruption was total. When a society institutionalizes the rejection of natural order, it reaches a point "beyond remedy" (2 Chronicles 36:16). The fire purges the land, removing the chaos so that order might eventually be replanted.

The Judgment of Ecclesiastical Disorder: Thyatira

The New Testament does not present a God who has softened His stance on order. In Revelation 2:18-29, Jesus addresses the church in Thyatira. While they are commended for their love and service, they are under the threat of severe judgment for a specific failure of hierarchy.

1. The Sin of Toleration "You tolerate that woman Jezebel, who calls herself a prophetess" (Revelation 2:20). The sin of the church leadership (the "angel" or messenger) was passivity. They allowed a woman to usurp the role of teacher and lead the servants of God into error. This mirrors the Ahab-Jezebel dynamic, where the male head abdicated his responsibility, allowing the female to rule and corrupt the house.

2. The Execution of Judgment Christ's response is terrifyingly active. He warns, "I will cast her onto a bed of sickness... Then I will strike her children dead" (Revelation 2:22-23). This is the Jesus of the New Testament speaking. He declares that He will kill the product of this disordered union (her "children," or followers) proving that He is "the One who searches minds and hearts" (Revelation 2:23). The church is not a democracy or a safe space for rebellion; it is a monarchy under the rule of Christ, and He actively purges those who subvert His order.

The Inevitability of the Harvest

These three witnesses establish that judgment is the immune response of a holy God to the infection of disorder.

1. **The Illusion of Delay** Because judgment does not always fall instantly, men assume it will never fall. Ecclesiastes 8:11 warns that when the sentence is not executed speedily, the hearts of men are fully set on doing evil. But as seen with Korah, Sodom, and Thyatira, the delay is not permission; it is patience. When patience expires, judgment is swift.

2. **The Restoration of Order** The purpose of these judgments is the restoration of order. By removing Korah, the priesthood was secured. By destroying Sodom, the moral pollution was checked. By judging Jezebel, the church is purified. We must understand that God values His order more than He values the comfort of those who rebel against it.

The Necessity of Fear and Order

We live in a time that mirrors the days of Lot and the rebellion of Korah. Authority is despised, nature is mocked, and the church tolerates Jezebel. We must not mistake God's silence for His approval. The Judge is at the door. The only safety from the coming storm is to be found within the House of Order, under the headship of Christ, living in obedience to His commands.

Having established the reality of judgment, we turn now to the hope of reconstruction. How do we rebuild the ruins? In the final section, we will examine the call to **Embracing God's Order** and the vision for a restored future.

Reflection Questions

1. How does the judgment of Korah (Numbers 16) refute the modern notion that all believers have equal authority to define doctrine and leadership?

2. In Revelation 2:20, why does Jesus hold the church responsible for "tolerating" Jezebel, and what does this imply about the duty of male leadership to silence false teaching?
3. How does the concept of "active judgment" (God striking) differ from the idea of "natural consequences," and why is this distinction vital for a biblical worldview?

> ***On Tolerance:*** *"Tolerance of disorder is not a virtue; it is a participation in the sin. The church at Thyatira was not judged for being unloving, but for being permissive."*
>
> ***On Judgment:*** *"God does not apologize for His judgments. He did not apologize to Sodom, He did not apologize to Korah, and He will not apologize to this generation. Order is the only shelter."*

Chapter 11: Conclusion - Embracing God's Order

11.1 - Final Exhortation

Return, Submit, Thrive The restoration of society, the church, and the home requires a deliberate, courageous return to the "Forgotten Order." This is not a call to cultural nostalgia but to structural obedience. Scripture reveals that submission is the prerequisite for spiritual authority. One cannot resist the chaos of the devil while living in rebellion against the order of God. To reject hierarchy is to invite the active opposition of God, but to align with His order is to secure the flow of His grace and protection. We must rebuild the ancient foundations to survive the coming storm.

🕮 THE WITNESSES

I. **James 4**
7: "Submit yourselves, then, to God. Resist the devil, and he will flee from you."

II. **Isaiah 58**
12: "Your people will rebuild the ancient ruins; you will restore the age-old foundations; you will be called Repairer of the Breach, Restorer of the Streets of Dwelling."

III. **1 Peter 5**
5: "Young men, in the same way, submit yourselves to your elders. And all of you, clothe yourselves with humility toward one another, because, 'God opposes the proud, but gives grace to the humble.'"

The Call to Return: Repairing the Breach

We live in a culture that treats the past as a prison and progress as the systematic dismantling of tradition. The modern mind assumes that the structures of the past were based on ignorance and oppression. However, Scripture describes a time when the foundations have been destroyed and the walls broken down, not by progress, but by rebellion. In such times, the man of God does not look forward to innovation. He looks backward to the "ancient ruins" to find the blueprint for survival.

1. Diagnosing the Breach Isaiah 58:12 speaks of a people who will be called "Repairer of the Breach." In the context of our study, the "breach" in our civilization is not merely economic or political. It is structural. The wall of Headship has been breached. The gate of Authority has been burned. When the father is removed from his post and the woman is removed from hers, the city lies open to attack. The breakdown of the family unit is the breach through which every other societal evil enters. To be a repairer is to re-establish the hierarchy of the home and the church according to God's original design in Genesis.

2. Seeking the Ancient Paths We do not need new theories on the sexes or the family. We need to "raise up the age-old foundations." This echoes the command in Jeremiah 6:16 to ask for the ancient paths. We must dig through the rubble of modern egalitarianism, feminism, and passivity to find the bedrock of creation order. We must return to the definitions God gave before the world fell. This return is an act of repentance. It is an admission that God's design was right, and our deviations were wrong.

The Call to Submit: The Mechanics of Spiritual Warfare

The modern mind recoils at the word "submit," viewing it as a position of weakness or inferiority. This reaction betrays a fundamental misunderstanding of biblical terminology. The Greek word used in James 4:7 is *hypotassō*. This is a military term that means "to arrange under" or "to fall into rank." It describes a tactical formation, not ontological value.

1. Tactical Alignment for Victory James connects submission directly to spiritual warfare: "Submit yourselves... Resist the devil." The word for "resist" is *anthistēmi*, which means to stand against or to withstand. The grammar implies a condition. You cannot successfully *anthistēmi* (resist) the enemy if you are not *hypotassō* (arranged under) the Commander. A soldier who breaks rank to fight alone has no authority and no cover. He is vulnerable. He disrupts the formation and endangers his unit.

2. No Authority Without Submission Many Christians attempt to rebuke the devil while living in rebellion against God's order in their homes. They claim authority over demons but refuse authority in their own lives. This is spiritual futility. Authority flows through order. If a wife rejects the headship of her husband, she steps out of the spiritual covering God has designed. If a husband refuses to submit to the headship of Christ, he leaves his family exposed. You cannot wield the sword of the Spirit effectively if you are standing outside of God's chain of command. Submission is the closing of the ranks. It brings the body into alignment so that the Head can direct the battle.

3. The Husband's Duty This military reality also reframes the husband's duty. He is not called to a position of privilege but to the front lines. When a man submits to Christ, he accepts the burden of leadership. He does not merely "die" in a passive sense; he lives as a poured-out offering. He stands between the enemy and his household. He bears the weight of provision, protection, and spiritual direction. This is active, burden-bearing headship. It is the fortification of the wall.

The Call to Thrive: The Danger of Divine Opposition

Order is not an end in itself. It is the environment in which life thrives. Conversely, disorder is the environment of death. 1 Peter

5:5 declares a universal principle that governs the universe: "God opposes the proud but gives grace to the humble."

1. God at War with the Proud The Greek word for "opposes" is *antitassetai*. This is a compound of *anti* (against) and *tassō* (to arrange). It is the precise opposite of *hypotassō*. It means that God "sets Himself in battle array against" the proud. This is a terrifying reality. The egalitarian spirit, which claims "I am equal in authority" and refuses to submit to appointed headship, is the essence of pride. It mimics the sin of Satan, who would not submit to his station. Those who subvert God's hierarchy do not merely face natural consequences. They face the active military resistance of God Himself. God lines up in battle against the disorder. A household built on rebellion is a household at war with its Creator.

2. The Flow of Grace On the other hand, grace (*charis*) is given to the humble. Grace is the divine power to function, to overcome, and to thrive. Grace flows downhill. It moves from the Father to the Son (1 Corinthians 11:3), from Christ to the man, and from the man to the woman. When we align ourselves under this flow through humility, we receive the power to function. A family operating according to God's hierarchy is a safe harbor. It is a place where the wife is protected, the children are nurtured, and the husband is empowered. This is the definition of thriving. It is life lived safely, productively, and joyfully because the walls are up and the gates are manned.

The Only Way Forward

The chaos of our time is the direct result of our rebellion against the Forgotten Order. We have broken the formation, and the enemy has flooded through the breach. The solution is not negotiation. The solution is not to soften the edges of truth to make it palatable to a rebellious culture. The solution is realignment.

We must return to the ancient foundations. We must submit to the divine hierarchy, not as a concession to power, but as a tactical necessity for spiritual survival. We must humble ourselves to receive the grace we so desperately need. The order has been forgotten by the world, but it must be remembered by the church. It waits for those with the courage to embrace it. Let us be the repairers of the breach. Let us return, submit, and thrive.

Reflection Questions

1. How does the military definition of *hypotassō* (to arrange under) change your understanding of submission from "weakness" to "tactical formation" in spiritual warfare?
2. In light of 1 Peter 5:5, how does the rejection of biblical roles constitute "pride," and what are the terrifying implications of God "setting Himself in battle array" (*antitassetai*) against a household?
3. What specific "ancient ruins" or "breaches" in your own family or community need to be repaired to restore God's intended protection against the enemy?

> ***On Formation:*** *"You cannot fight the devil while fighting God's order. Submission is not about losing your voice; it is about finding your rank. A soldier out of rank is not a hero; he is a casualty."*
>
> ***On Reconstruction:*** *"We are not called to invent a new way to live; we are called to clear the rubble. The foundation of God stands sure. We must simply have the humility to build upon it again."*

receive the grace we so desperately need. The order has been forgotten by the world, but it must be remembered by the church. [illegible] to those with the courage to remember it. Let us go [illegible] against the [illegible], let us remain submitted and thrive.

[illegible]

1. How does the military definition of *hupotassō* (to arrange under) change your understanding of submission from "weakness" to "tactical formation" in spiritual warfare?
2. In light of [illegible], how does the function of biblical roles constitute "guides" and what are the terrifying implications of God "setting Himself in battle array" (*antitassō*) against a household [illegible]?
3. What specific "broken" ranks of [illegible] in your own family or community need to be re-ordered to restore God's intended protection against the enemy?

On Formation: *You cannot fight the devil while defying the order.* Submission is not about losing your voice; it is about finding your position. A soldier out of rank is not a hero; he is a casualty.

On Restoration: [illegible] to be [illegible] the [illegible]. The [illegible] of God [illegible] same. We must simply come the humility to fall into position.

11.2 - A Vision for the Future Church

Restored Order, Revived Mission The restoration of the church and its mission to the nations depends entirely on the recovery of the "Forgotten Order." A church that reflects the chaos of the culture cannot convert the culture. Scripture reveals that the Church is the "household of God," structured by divine conduct rather than human preference. The credibility of the Word of God is tethered to the order of our families. We must rebuild the internal structure of headship and submission so that the body may grow and the truth may stand firm.

🕮 THE WITNESSES

I. **1 Timothy 3**
15: "in case I am delayed, so that you will know how each one must conduct himself in God's household, which is the church of the living God, the pillar and foundation of the truth."

II. **Titus 2**
5: "to be self-controlled, pure, managers of their households, kind, and submissive to their own husbands, so that the word of God will not be discredited."

III. **Ephesians 4**
16: "From Him the whole body, fitted and held together by every supporting ligament, grows and builds itself up in love through the work of each individual part."

The Ecclesiastical Architecture: Order as Foundation

The modern church often views itself as a volunteer organization or a spiritual service provider to be shaped by market trends. However, Paul defines it in 1 Timothy 3:15 as "God's household." This metaphor is not accidental. It implies that the church is a family unit writ large. It is governed by the Father's rules and not the members' votes.

1. Conduct is Prescribed Paul writes so that Timothy will know "how people ought to conduct themselves." The behavior within the church is not left to cultural whims or pragmatic innovation. It is prescribed by the Head of the house. This conduct includes the qualifications for elders and deacons (1 Timothy 3:1-13) which are rooted in the management of their own households. A disordered home disqualifies a man from leading God's home. The structure of the church must mirror the structure of the creation order.

2. The Pillar of Truth The church is called the "pillar and foundation of the truth" (1 Timothy 3:15). A pillar holds up the roof. A foundation supports the structure. If the order of the church collapses, the "truth" it upholds crashes to the ground in the eyes of the world. We cannot uphold the truth of the Gospel while dismantling the structure God built to support it. When the church abandons the distinctions of men and women, it removes the pillar. The truth remains true, but it is no longer held high for the world to see.

The Missional Veto: Why Order Matters

The connection between our private lives and our public witness is forged in Titus 2:5. Paul instructs older women to train the younger women in specific domestic duties, culminating in the command to be "submissive to their own husbands." The reason given is terrifying in its stakes. It is "so that the word of God will not be discredited."

1. The Danger of Blasphemy The word "discredited" (Greek *blasphēmeō*) means to be blasphemed or spoken against. When a Christian wife rejects the headship of her husband, or when a home is chaotic and ungoverned, the outside world blasphemes the Word of God. They conclude that the Gospel has no power to order life. Our rebellion gives the enemy ammunition. A church filled with egalitarian marriages is a church that has disarmed itself before the world. It preaches a Lord who cannot even rule His own people.

2. The Argument of Order Conversely, a home operating according to God's hierarchy is a fortress of peace in a world of war. It is an irrefutable argument for the Lordship of Christ. When men lead with sacrificial love and women respond with reverent submission, the Gospel is adorned (Titus 2:10). The future church will win the world not by mimicking its feminism, but by presenting the stark contrast of biblical order. The beauty of hierarchy is the greatest apologetic against the chaos of autonomy.

Organic Growth: The Mechanics of the Body

Order is not static. It is the mechanism of growth. Ephesians 4:16 describes the body as "fitted and held together by every supporting ligament."

1. Connection Requires Order A ligament connects bone to bone. It provides stability and allows movement. In the body of Christ, these ligaments represent the relationships of authority and submission. This applies to pastors and people, husbands and wives, parents and children. If the ligaments are severed or loose, the body becomes spastic and paralyzed. It cannot move. An egalitarian body is a disjointed body. It cannot function because the parts refuse to align.

2. Growth Through Work The text says the body grows "through the work of each individual part." The parts can only do their work if they are in their proper place. An eye cannot function as a hand. A woman cannot function as a father. A man cannot function as a mother. When we accept our God-given stations, the "energy" (Greek *energeia*) flows. The body builds itself up in love. Growth is the result of structure. If we want the future church to grow in power and maturity, we must return to the structure of the New Testament.

Building for the Future

The "Forgotten Order" is not a relic of the past to be studied in a museum. It is the blueprint for the future church. As the culture collapses under the weight of its own rebellion, the church must stand firm. It must be established on the foundation of God's Word, modeled after His household, and adorned with the beauty of holiness.

We must build houses, families, and churches that reflect this order. We must reject the chaos of egalitarianism and embrace the strength of hierarchy. We must realize that our submission is our warfare and our order is our witness. When we do this, the church will rise as the pillar of truth, holding high the light of Christ in a darkening world. The gates of hell will not prevail against it.

Reflection Questions

1. How does 1 Timothy 3:15 challenge the modern notion that church structure can be adapted to fit cultural preferences? What does "God's household" imply about authority?

2. According to Titus 2:5, what is the direct link between a wife's submission and the reputation of the Gospel? How does disorder "blaspheme" the Word?

3. In light of Ephesians 4:16, why is the proper "work of each individual part." (defined by role) essential for the growth of the body?

> ***On Witness:*** *"The world is watching our homes. If our theology doesn't work at the dinner table, it won't work in the public square. Order is our greatest apologetic."*
>
> ***On Structure:*** *"You cannot have the life of the body without the structure of the skeleton. Remove the hierarchy, and you don't get freedom. You get a heap of bones."*

Appendix

A.1: Hebrew and Greek Terms

This glossary defines the core vocabulary used throughout this book to establish the biblical doctrine of hierarchy, gender, and order. The definitions below are derived from the Berean Standard Bible and its underlying manuscript data.

Each entry includes the Strong's Number, the translation, a theological definition, and the specific chapters in this book where the term is applied.

I. Hebrew Terms (Old Testament)

1. Cherem (חֵרֶם)

- **Strong's Number:** H2764
- **Translation:** Devoted to destruction / Ban / Curse
- **Definition:** Something devoted to God, often for destruction; a ban. It refers to the total removal or cursing of a thing or people due to violation of God's covenant order.
- **Biblical Witness:**
    - **Malachi 4:6:** "... or else I will come and strike the land with a **curse** (*cherem*)."
- **Book References:**
    - 10.1 - Societal Chaos and Fatherlessness

2. Ezer (עֵזֶר)

- **Strong's Number:** H5828
- **Translation:** Helper / Help
- **Definition:** Essential aid or succor. It describes one who supplies strength where it is lacking. It is frequently applied to God as the "Helper" of Israel (e.g., Psalm 33:20), proving the term carries no connotation of ontological inferiority.

However, in the context of marriage (Genesis 2:18), it functions within the hierarchy of the husband's headship as the one who supplies what the man lacks to fulfill the dominion mandate.

- **Biblical Witness:**
    - **Genesis 2:18:** "I will make him a **helper** (*ezer*) suitable for him."
- **Book References:**
    - 1.2 - Woman as Subordinate Helper
    - 4.1 - Pre-Fall Harmony
    - 5.4 - The Principle of Witnesses in Action
    - 9.3 - Abigail's Wisdom in Submission
    - 9.4 - Rebellion's Folly

3. Ichabod (אִי־כָבוֹד)

- **Strong's Number:** H350
- **Translation:** No Glory / Glory has departed
- **Definition:** A compound word meaning "Where is the glory?" or "The glory is not." It signifies the removal of God's weighty presence due to the corruption of leadership and the profaning of what is holy.
- **Biblical Witness:**
    - **1 Samuel 4:21:** "She named the boy **Ichabod**, saying, 'The glory has departed from Israel'..."
- **Book References:**
    - 10.1 - Societal Chaos and Fatherlessness

4. Ish (אִישׁ)

- **Strong's Number:** H376

- **Translation:** Man / Husband
- **Definition:** A man, husband, or individual; a male. It denotes the male in distinction to the female (*ishshah*).
- **Biblical Witness:**
    - **Genesis 2:23:** "... she shall be called 'Woman,' for she was taken out of **Man** (*ish*)."
- **Book References:**
    - 1.2 - Woman as Subordinate Helper

5. Ishshah (אִשָּׁה)

- **Strong's Number:** H802
- **Translation:** Woman / Wife
- **Definition:** A woman, wife, or female. Created from the man (*ish*), establishing her derivation and functional subordination.
- **Biblical Witness:**
    - **Genesis 2:22:** "Then the LORD God made a **woman** (*ishshah*) from the rib He had taken out of the man..."
- **Book References:**
    - 1.2 - Woman as Subordinate Helper

6. Kenegdo (כְּנֶגְדּוֹ)

- **Strong's Number:** H5048 (Root: *Neged*)
- **Translation:** Suitable for him / Corresponding to him
- **Definition:** Literally "like opposite him" or "corresponding to him." It defines the woman as the man's equal counterpart in essence (ontological equality), facing him as a mirror, yet created to help him.

- **Biblical Witness:**
    - **Genesis 2:18:** "... a helper **suitable for him** (*kenegdo*)."
- **Book References:**
    - 1.2 - Woman as Subordinate Helper

7. Mashal (מָשַׁל)

- **Strong's Number:** H4910
- **Translation:** Rule / Master
- **Definition:** To rule, have dominion, reign. It describes the husband's authority, which became a point of conflict (*teshuqah*) after the Fall.
- **Biblical Witness:**
    - **Genesis 3:16:** "... Your desire will be for your husband, and he will **rule over** (*mashal*) you."
- **Book References:**
    - 4.2 - Post-Fall Consequences
    - 6.1 - Old Testament Patterns
    - 7.4 - Societal Collapses from Inversion

8. Neged (נֶגֶד)

- **Strong's Number:** H5048
- **Translation:** Opposite / In front of
- **Definition:** That which is conspicuous or in front of; a counterpart.
- **Biblical Witness:**
    - **Joshua 3:16:** "... the waters ... stood up in a heap ... **opposite** (*neged*) Jericho."

- **Book References:**
    - 4.1 - Pre-Fall Harmony

9. Oto (אתוֹ)

- **Strong's Number:** H853 (Direct Object Marker) + Suffix
- **Translation:** Him
- **Definition:** The singular masculine object marker. Used in Genesis 1:27 to show that *Ha'adam* (the man/mankind) was created singular ("Him") before being differentiated as male and female.
- **Biblical Witness:**
    - **Genesis 1:27:** "... in the image of God He created **him** (*oto*)..."
- **Book References:**
    - 3.1 - Genesis 1v27 and 9v6 Exegeted

10. Otam (אֹתָם)

- **Strong's Number:** H853 (Direct Object Marker) + Suffix
- **Translation:** Them
- **Definition:** The plural object marker. Used in Genesis 1:27 to show the plurality of the species ("Them") as male and female.
- **Biblical Witness:**
    - **Genesis 1:27:** "... male and female He created **them** (*otam*)."
- **Book References:**
    - 3.1 - Genesis 1v27 and 9v6 Exegeted

11. Teshuqah (תְּשׁוּקָה)

- **Strong's Number:** H8669

- **Translation:** Desire
- **Definition:** A longing or desire; specifically, a desire to control or master. In Genesis 3:16 and 4:7, it indicates a conflict where the subordinate desires to usurp the authority of the head.
- **Biblical Witness:**
    - **Genesis 4:7:** "... sin is crouching at the door. Its **desire** (*teshuqah*) is for you, but you must master it."
- **Book References:**
    - 1.2 - Woman as Subordinate Helper
    - 4.2 - Post-Fall Consequences
    - 7.1 - Feminist Errors in Context
    - 7.4 - Societal Collapses from Inversion

12. Tselem (צֶלֶם)

- **Strong's Number:** H6754
- **Translation:** Image
- **Definition:** A representative figure, image, or likeness. Establishes the *Ontological Equality* of male and female.
- **Biblical Witness:**
    - **Genesis 1:27:** "So God created man in His own **image** (*tselem*)..."
- **Book References:**
    - 3.1 - Genesis 1v27 and 9v6 Exegeted

II. Greek Terms (New Testament)

13. Akyron (ἀκυρόω / ἄκυρος)

- **Strong's Number:** G194 (verb: *akyroō*)
- **Translation:** Nullify / Make void
- **Definition:** To invalidate, deprive of force and authority.
- **Biblical Witness:**
    - **Matthew 15:6:** "Thus you **nullify** (*ēkyrōsate*) the word of God for the sake of your tradition."
- **Book References:**
    - 7.2 - Philosophers' Partial Truths

14. Anthistēmi (ἀνθίστημι)

- **Strong's Number:** G436
- **Translation:** Oppose / Resist
- **Definition:** To set one's self against; to withstand.
- **Biblical Witness:**
    - **2 Timothy 3:8:** "Just as Jannes and Jambres **opposed** (*antestēsan*) Moses..."
- **Book References:**
    - 11.1 - Final Exhortation

15. Antitassetai (ἀντιτάσσω)

- **Strong's Number:** G498
- **Translation:** Opposes / Resists
- **Definition:** To range in battle against; to oppose one's self to.
- **Biblical Witness:**
    - **James 4:6:** "God **opposes** (*antitassetai*) the proud but gives grace to the humble."
- **Book References:**

- 11.1 - Final Exhortation

16. Authentein (αὐθεντεῖν)

- **Strong's Number:** G831
- **Translation:** To exercise authority
- **Definition:** To govern, exercise dominion, or act as an autocrat. Paul forbids a woman to *authentein* a man in the church assembly.
- **Biblical Witness:**
  - **1 Timothy 2:12:** "I do not permit a woman ... **to exercise authority over** (*authentein*) a man..."
- **Book References:**
  - 6.2 - Prophecy vs Teaching
  - 8.1 - Debunking Egalitarian Arguments
  - 8.4 - Prophecy vs Teaching in Modern Ministry

17. Blasphēmeō (βλασφημέω)

- **Strong's Number:** G987
- **Translation:** Blaspheme / Slander / Malign
- **Definition:** To speak reproachfully, rail at, or revile.
- **Biblical Witness:**
  - **Titus 2:5:** "... so that the word of God will not be **maligned** (*blasphēmētai*)."
- **Book References:**
  - 11.2 - A Vision for the Future Church

18. Charis (χάρις)

- **Strong's Number:** G5485
- **Translation:** Grace

- **Definition:** That which affords joy, pleasure, delight; unmerited favor.
- **Biblical Witness:**
    - **2 Timothy 1:2:** "**Grace** (*charis*), mercy, and peace from God the Father..."
- **Book References:**
    - 11.1 - Final Exhortation

19. Didaskein / Didaskō (διδάσκω)

- **Strong's Number:** G1321
- **Translation:** To teach
- **Definition:** To hold a discourse with others in order to instruct them; to impart doctrine.
- **Biblical Witness:**
    - **1 Timothy 2:12:** "I do not permit a woman **to teach** (*didaskein*)..."
- **Book References:**
    - 6.2 - Prophecy vs Teaching
    - 8.4 - Prophecy vs Teaching in Modern Ministry

20. Energeia (ἐνέργεια)

- **Strong's Number:** G1753
- **Translation:** Working / Power
- **Definition:** Operative power, efficiency, energy.
- **Biblical Witness:**
    - **Philippians 3:21:** "... by the **power** (*energeian*) that enables Him to bring everything under His control."

- **Book References:**
    - 11.2 - A Vision for the Future Church

21. Gnosis (γνῶσις)

- **Strong's Number:** G1108
- **Translation:** Knowledge
- **Definition:** Knowledge signifies in general intelligence, understanding. Used in context of "false knowledge" (Gnosticism).
- **Biblical Witness:**
    - **1 Timothy 6:20:** "... opposing arguments of so-called **knowledge** (*gnōseōs*)."
- **Book References:**
    - 7.6 - Early Church vs Proto-Egalitarianism

22. Graphe (γραφή)

- **Strong's Number:** G1124
- **Translation:** Scripture
- **Definition:** A writing, thing written; specifically, Holy Scripture.
- **Biblical Witness:**
    - **2 Timothy 3:16:** "All **Scripture** (*graphē*) is God-breathed..."
- **Book References:**
    - 5.1 - Jesus Upholds the Law
    - 5.2 - Paul's Authority as Scripture

23. Hupotasso / Hypotassō (ὑποτάσσω)

- **Strong's Number:** G5293

- **Translation:** Submit / Subject
- **Definition:** A military term meaning to arrange under; to subordinate; to submit to one's control.
- **Biblical Witness:**
    - **Colossians 3:18:** "Wives, **submit** (*hypotassesthe*) to your husbands, as is fitting in the Lord."
- **Book References:**
    - 7.3 - Church Leaders' Reflections on Order
    - 8.6 - Anticipating the Assault
    - 11.1 - Final Exhortation

24. Kephale (κεφαλή)

- **Strong's Number:** G2776
- **Translation:** Head
- **Definition:** The literal head; metaphorically, the source or authority figure. In biblical hierarchy, it denotes the superior position in a functional relationship.
- **Biblical Witness:**
    - **1 Corinthians 11:3:** "... the **head** (*kephalē*) of every man is Christ, and the **head** (*kephalē*) of the woman is man..."
- **Book References:**
    - 5.4 - The Principle of Witnesses in Action
    - 7.3 - Church Leaders' Reflections on Order
    - 8.1 - Debunking Egalitarian Arguments
    - 8.6 - Anticipating the Assault

25. Logos (λόγος)

- **Strong's Number:** G3056
- **Translation:** Word
- **Definition:** A word, uttered by a living voice; the essential Word of God, Jesus Christ.
- **Biblical Witness:**
    - **John 1:1:** "In the beginning was the **Word** (*Logos*)..."
- **Book References:**
    - 5.1 - Jesus Upholds the Law

26. Lythēnai (λυθῆναι)

- **Strong's Number:** G3089 (Root: *Lyō*)
- **Translation:** Broken
- **Definition:** To loosen, unbind, break, or annul.
- **Biblical Witness:**
    - **John 10:35:** "... and the Scripture cannot **be broken** (*lythēnai*)..."
- **Book References:**
    - 5.1 - Jesus Upholds the Law

27. Oikourgos (οἰκουργός)

- **Strong's Number:** G3635
- **Translation:** Workers at home / Keepers at home
- **Definition:** Caring for the house, working at home.
- **Biblical Witness:**
    - **Titus 2:5:** "... to be self-controlled, pure, **managers of their homes** (*oikourgous*)..."
- **Book References:**

- 7.1 - Feminist Errors in Context
- 9.2 - Titus 2 Older Women Training the Younger

28. Philandros (φίλανδρος)

- **Strong's Number:** G5362
- **Translation:** Loving their husbands
- **Definition:** Affectionate to one's husband.
- **Biblical Witness:**
  - **Titus 2:4:** "... train the younger women **to love their husbands** (*philandrous*)..."
- **Book References:**
  - 9.2 - Titus 2 Older Women Training the Younger

29. Philoteknos (φιλότεκνος)

- **Strong's Number:** G5388
- **Translation:** Loving their children
- **Definition:** Fond of one's children.
- **Biblical Witness:**
  - **Titus 2:4:** "... to love their husbands and **to love their children** (*philoteknous*)..."
- **Book References:**
  - 9.2 - Titus 2 Older Women Training the Younger

30. Skolios (σκολιός)

- **Strong's Number:** G4646
- **Translation:** Crooked / Warped / Harsh
- **Definition:** Crooked, curved; metaphorically, perverse, wicked, or unfair/harsh.

- **Biblical Witness:**
    - **1 Peter 2:18:** "... not only to those who are good and gentle, but also to those who are **harsh** (*skoliois*)."
- **Book References:**
    - 9.5 - Practical Obedience Under Fire

31. Synklēronomois (συγκληρονόμος)

- **Strong's Number:** G4789
- **Translation:** Co-heirs / Heirs together
- **Definition:** A fellow heir, a joint heir; one who obtains something assigned to himself with others.
- **Biblical Witness:**
    - **1 Peter 3:7:** "... treat them with respect as **heirs with you** (*synklēronomois*) of the gracious gift of life..."
- **Book References:**
    - 3.2 - Positional Inferiority, Not Ontological

32. Tassō (τάσσω)

- **Strong's Number:** G5021
- **Translation:** Ordained / Instituted
- **Definition:** To place in a certain order, to arrange, to assign a place, to appoint.
- **Biblical Witness:**
    - **Romans 13:1:** "... the authorities that exist have been **instituted** (*tetagmenai*) by God."
- **Book References:**
    - 11.1 - Final Exhortation

33. Taxis (τάξις)

- **Strong's Number:** G5010
- **Translation:** Order
- **Definition:** An arranging, arrangement, order; a fixed succession observing a fixed time.
- **Biblical Witness:**
    - **1 Corinthians 14:40:** "But everything must be done properly and in **order** (*taxin*)."
- **Book References:**
    - 1.2 - Woman as Subordinate Helper

III. Terms Grouped by Theological Category

The following list reorganizes the glossary terms into theological categories. See how specific words function together to establish the arguments presented in the book.

1. Creation Order & Ontology (Design) These terms describe the foundational state of humanity before the Fall, establishing the equality of essence and the distinction of roles.

- *Tselem* (Image): Equality of essence.
- *Ish / Ishshah* (Man / Woman): Differentiation.
- *Oto / Otam* (Him / Them): Unity and Plurality.
- *Ezer* (Helper): Essential aid.
- *Kenegdo* (Suitable): Corresponding counterpart.
- *Synklēronomois* (Co-heirs): Spiritual equality.

2. Hierarchy & Authority (Function) These terms describe the flow of authority and the structure of relationships within God's design.

- *Kephale* (Head): Source and Authority.

- *Taxis* (Order): Arrangement.
- *Tassō* (Ordained): Appointed by God.
- *Authentein* (Exercise Authority): Governing power.
- *Didaskein* (To Teach): Authoritative instruction.
- *Mashal* (Rule): Dominion (often in a post-Fall context).

3. Submission & Domestic Order (Response) These terms describe the righteous response to authority and the management of the home.

- *Hupotasso* (Submit): Voluntary alignment under authority.
- *Oikourgos* (Workers at home): Domestic orientation.
- *Philandros* (Loving husbands): Affectionate loyalty.
- *Philoteknos* (Loving children): Maternal care.

4. The Fall & Conflict (Corruption) These terms describe the distortion of God's order due to sin.

- *Teshuqah* (Desire): The urge to control/usurp.
- *Skolios* (Harsh): Crooked authority.
- *Anthistēmi* (Oppose): Resisting established order.
- *Blasphēmeō* (Malign): Speaking evil of the Word.

5. Judgment & Truth (Consequences) These terms relate to the defense of truth and the consequences of abandoning it.

- *Cherem* (Devoted to destruction): The ban/curse.
- *Ichabod* (Glory departed): Loss of God's presence.
- *Graphe* (Scripture): The standard of truth.
- *Akyron* (Nullify): Making void the Word.
- *Gnosis* (Knowledge): False knowledge/Gnosticism.

A.2: Index of Scripture References

This index lists the specific Bible verses addressed in *The Forgotten Order*. Citations include the chapter number and title to indicate the theological context in which the verse is applied.

Old Testament

Genesis

- **2:17**:
  - **1.1** (Man's Firstness and Authority)
  - **1.2** (Woman as Subordinate Helper)
  - **4.1** (Pre-Fall Harmony)
  - **4.2** (Post-Fall Consequences)
- **2:18**:
  - **1.2** (Woman as Subordinate Helper)
  - **4.1** (Pre-Fall Harmony)
  - **5.4** (The Principle of Witnesses in Action)
  - **7.2** (Philosophers' Partial Truths)
- **2:19**:
  - **1.1** (Man's Firstness and Authority)
  - **1.2** (Woman as Subordinate Helper)
- **2:20**:
  - **1.1** (Man's Firstness and Authority)
- **2:22**:
  - **1.2** (Woman as Subordinate Helper)
  - **2.1** (The Father's Chain of Headship)
  - **3.1** (Genesis 1v27 and 9v6 Exegeted)
- **2:23**:
  - **1.2** (Woman as Subordinate Helper)
- **2:24**:
  - **5.1** (Jesus Upholds the Law)
- **3:2**:
  - **4.1** (Pre-Fall Harmony)

1 Kings

- **21:7–25**:
  - **8.3** (Negative Biblical Examples)
  - **9.4** (Rebellion's Folly)

2 Kings

- **22:14**:
  - **6.1** (Old Testament Patterns)

2 Chronicles

- **36:16**:
  - **10.2** (Divine Judgment in Scripture)

Psalm

- **115:9**:
  - **1.2** (Woman as Subordinate Helper)

Proverbs

- **17:6**:
  - **10.1** (Societal Chaos and Fatherlessness)
- **31:11–30**:
  - **9.1** (Proverbs 31 Strength in Submission)

Ecclesiastes

- **8:11**:
  - **10.2** (Divine Judgment in Scripture)

Isaiah

- **3:2**:
  - **7.4** (Societal Collapses from Inversion)
- **3:12**:

- **9.4** (Rebellion's Folly)

Malachi

- **4:6**:
  - **7.4** (Societal Collapses from Inversion)
  - **10.1** (Societal Chaos and Fatherlessness)

New Testament

Matthew

- **5:17**:
  - **5.1** (Jesus Upholds the Law)
  - **5.4** (The Principle of Witnesses in Action)
- **5:18**:
  - **5.1** (Jesus Upholds the Law)
- **18:16**:
  - **5.4** (The Principle of Witnesses in Action)
- **19:4**:
  - **5.1** (Jesus Upholds the Law)
  - **5.4** (The Principle of Witnesses in Action)
- **19:8**:
  - **5.1** (Jesus Upholds the Law)

John

- **6:38**:
  - **2.1** (The Father's Chain of Headship)
  - **5.1** (Jesus Upholds the Law)
  - **5.4** (The Principle of Witnesses in Action)
  - **6.3** (New Testament Continuity)

Colossians

- **3:11**:
  - **2.2** (Refuting Egalitarian Claims)
  - **3.2** (Positional Inferiority, Not Ontological)
- **3:18**:
  - **2.2** (Refuting Egalitarian Claims)
- **3:22**:
  - **2.2** (Refuting Egalitarian Claims)

1 Timothy

- **2:12**:
  - **1.1** (Man's Firstness and Authority)
  - **2.2** (Refuting Egalitarian Claims)
  - **5.2** (Paul's Authority as Scripture)
  - **6.2** (Prophecy vs Teaching)
  - **7.3** (Church Leaders' Reflections on Order)
  - **7.5** (The Early Church on Hierarchy)
  - **7.6** (Early Church vs Proto-Egalitarianism)
  - **8.1** (Debunking Egalitarian Arguments)
  - **8.4** (Prophecy vs Teaching in Modern Ministry)
  - **8.6** (Anticipating the Assault)
  - **9.2** (Titus 2 Older Women Training the Younger)
  - **9.5** (Practical Obedience Under Fire)
- **2:13**:
  - **1.1** (Man's Firstness and Authority)
  - **1.2** (Woman as Subordinate Helper)
  - **2.2** (Refuting Egalitarian Claims)

- **2.1** (The Father's Chain of Headship)
- **5.1** (Jesus Upholds the Law)
- **5.2** (Paul's Authority as Scripture)
- **5.3** (Addressing Common Attacks on Paul's Apostleship)

Revelation

- **2:18–29**:
  - **10.2** (Divine Judgment in Scripture)

A.3: An Invitation to the Reader

Entering God's Order If you have read this book as someone who does not yet follow Jesus Christ, you may have found the descriptions of biblical order, hierarchy, and family structure challenging. You may see the logic of a designed universe yet feel powerless or unsure how to live it out. You may feel the weight of the law: the requirement of perfection and submission, knowing that you fall short.

This book has argued that the universe operates on a specific design: God → Christ → Man → Woman.

However, if you are not "in Christ," you are currently disconnected from this source of life and order. The Bible is clear that those outside of Christ are not merely "disordered" or "confused." They are spiritually dead and under the judgment of God. To experience the victory and peace described in these pages, you must first address your standing before the Creator.

1. The Reality of Disorder (Sin)

The chaos you see in the world, and likely feel in your own heart, is the result of humanity rejecting God's authority. This is the ultimate subversion of hierarchy. Sin is not just a mistake or a lapse in judgment; it is cosmic treason. It is the creature saying to the Creator, "I am the head. You are not needed."

Because God is the source of all life and order, to cut yourself off from Him through rebellion is to choose death and chaos.

- **Romans 3:23:** "for all have sinned and fall short of the glory of God"
- **Isaiah 59:2:** "But your iniquities have built barriers between you and your God, and your sins have hidden His face from you, so that He does not hear."

2. The Impossibility of Self-Restoration

You cannot restore order to your life by simply trying harder to be a "good person" or a "good spouse." The standard of God's order is absolute perfection. God is holy, and He cannot look upon iniquity with favor. Therefore, your best efforts are insufficient to repair the breach caused by your rebellion.

- **Romans 3:10:** "As it is written: 'There is no one righteous, not even one.'"
- **James 2:10:** "Whoever keeps the whole law but stumbles at just one point is guilty of breaking all of it."

Without intervention, you remain under the wrath of God; destined for a place prepared for the devil and his angels. It was never meant for you. You are separated from the very design that sustains the universe, but you don't have to be.

- **Matthew 25:41:** "Then He will say to those on His left, `Depart from Me, you who are cursed, into the eternal fire prepared for the devil and his angels."
- **John 3:36:** "Whoever believes in the Son has eternal life. Whoever rejects the Son will not see life. Instead, the wrath of God remains on him."

3. The Divine Solution (The Gospel)

God, in His mercy, did not leave us in chaos. He sent His Son, Jesus Christ, to reestablish the link between God and man. Jesus is the only one who lived in perfect submission to the Father. He established the model of hierarchy by submitting His will entirely to His Father, God.

Jesus took upon Himself the penalty for our rebellion. On the cross, He absorbed the chaos and judgment due to us. He satisfied the justice of God so that mercy could be extended to us.

- **Romans 5:8:** "But God proves His love for us in this: While we were still sinners, Christ died for us."
- **1 Peter 3:18:** "For Christ also suffered for sins once for all, the righteous for the unrighteous, to bring you to God..."

By His resurrection, He proved He has the power to bring life out of death and order out of disorder.

4. How to Respond: Entering the Order of Christ

Salvation is the ultimate act of submission. It is acknowledging that you are not the head. It is admitting that you are not the authority. It is confessing that you have rebelled and that you need a Savior.

If you recognize your need for Christ, the Bible provides a clear path to reconciliation. It is not about earning your way back; it is about receiving what Christ has done.

A. Repent of Your Rebellion To repent means to change your mind: to turn away from your sin and self-rule and turn toward God. You must admit that your way has failed and that God's way is right.

- **Acts 3:19:** "Repent, then, and turn back, so that your sins may be wiped away,"

B. Believe in the Lord Jesus Belief is more than intellectual agreement. It is a reliance on Jesus alone for your standing before God. It is trusting that His death paid for your sin and His resurrection secured your life.

- **Acts 16:31:** "...Believe in the Lord Jesus, and you will be saved, you and your household."
- **John 20:31:** "But these are written so that you may believe that Jesus is the Christ, the Son of God, and that by believing you may have life in His name."

C. Confess Him as Head and Lord You must verbalize your allegiance. To call Jesus "Lord" is to place yourself under His absolute authority. It is the restoration of the hierarchy that was broken in Eden.

- **Romans 10:9:** “that if you confess with your mouth, ‘Jesus is Lord,’ and believe in your heart that God raised Him from the dead, you will be saved.”

5. Your Invitation

To walk in the victory described in this book, you must first be born again. You must be grafted into the Chain of Headship through Christ. Without Him, you have no power to love your wife as Christ loved the church, nor to submit to your husband as to the Lord.

Do not let this moment pass. The order of the universe testifies against rebellion, but the blood of Christ testifies to His mercy. Call upon Him. Ask Jesus to be Lord of your life, while there’s still time.